KENNETH CRAGG ON THE INTERSECTION OF FAITHS

Volume 2

THE THEOLOGY OF UNITY

THE THEOLOGY OF UNITY

MUḤAMMAD 'ABDUH

Translated from the Arabic
by Isḥāq Musa'ad and Kenneth Cragg

LONDON AND NEW YORK

First published in 1966 by George Allen & Unwin Ltd.

This edition first published in 2022
by Routledge
2 Park Square, Milton Park, Abingdon, Oxon OX14 4RN

and by Routledge
605 Third Avenue, New York, NY 10158

Routledge is an imprint of the Taylor & Francis Group, an informa business

© 1966 George Allen & Unwin Ltd

All rights reserved. No part of this book may be reprinted or reproduced or utilised in any form or by any electronic, mechanical, or other means, now known or hereafter invented, including photocopying and recording, or in any information storage or retrieval system, without permission in writing from the publishers.

Trademark notice: Product or corporate names may be trademarks or registered trademarks, and are used only for identification and explanation without intent to infringe.

British Library Cataloguing in Publication Data
A catalogue record for this book is available from the British Library

ISBN: 978-1-03-218552-1 (Set)
ISBN: 978-1-03-218560-6 (Set) (ebk)
ISBN: 978-1-03-218489-0 (Volume 2) (hbk)
ISBN: 978-1-03-218513-2 (Volume 2) (pbk)
ISBN: 978-1-00-325485-0 (Volume 2) (ebk)

DOI: 10.4324/9781003254850

Publisher's Note
The publisher has gone to great lengths to ensure the quality of this reprint but points out that some imperfections in the original copies may be apparent.

Disclaimer
The publisher has made every effort to trace copyright holders and would welcome correspondence from those they have been unable to trace.

THE THEOLOGY OF UNITY

BY

MUHAMMAD 'ABDUH

TRANSLATED FROM THE ARABIC BY
ISHĀQ MUSA'AD
AND
KENNETH CRAGG

London
GEORGE ALLEN & UNWIN LTD
RUSKIN HOUSE · MUSEUM STREET

FIRST PUBLISHED IN 1966

This book is copyright under the Berne Convention. Apart from any fair dealing for the purposes of private study, research, criticism or review, as permitted under the Copyright Act, 1956, no portion may be reproduced by any process without written permission. Enquiries should be addressed to the publishers.

© *George Allen & Unwin Ltd.*, 1966

PRINTED IN GREAT BRITAIN
in 11 on 12 point *Old Style* type by
UNWIN BROTHERS LTD
WOKING AND LONDON

Foreword

That translation always constitutes an urge and an occasion for collaboration is familiar enough to all who have attempted it. No single individual has two native tongues. Where two languages come together it is well there should be two, to either 'manner born'. The degree of mutuality may vary: the need for it is perpetual.

The reasons for desiring an English version of Muḥammad 'Abduh's *Risālat al-Tauḥīd* are sufficiently argued in the Introduction that follows and justified in the text itself. The circumstances that brought together the two translators are simple—a year's joint residence in St. Augustine's College, Canterbury, England, where each man normally undertakes a sustained piece of academic work assigned for his year's energies among more general studies. It seemed natural for an Egyptian, serving within the Christian Ministry, to concern himself with a modern theological work that has played a conspicuous part in the twentieth century development of theological activity within the faith of the vast majority of his fellow countrymen. It seemed equally natural for an Englishman, committed for many years to the business of Muslim–Christian studies, to lend his hand on his side of such a transaction. The result is this rendering. We have been grateful for the chance to consult B. Michel and M. 'Abd al-Rāziq's French version, (1925), long out of print. But the English text derives from 'Abduh's Arabic in the eighteenth edition, with annotations by Rashīd Riḍā.

Our hope is that the enterprise of an English translation may be a token of wider fields of Anglo-Egyptian comradeship and a means to the hopeful, and still arduous, purpose of Muslim–Christian interpretation.

Canterbury, 1964

ISHĀQ MUSA'AD
KENNETH CRAGG

Introduction

'I went through many unfamiliar streets for what seemed a long time. At length we came to a large building and my father told me that it was Al-Azhar—a mysterious quantity. I was still to learn what that name would mean to me and had no inkling of the patterns and procedures, the workings and prospects of life within it. In bewildered apprehension I heard a strange noise at the gate, a buzzing like that of bees, the sort of noise which strikes the ear but cannot be distinguished into articulate sounds. What I heard filled me with misgiving. I saw my father take off his shoes at the gate and take them, folded, into his hand. Following suit, I went forward with him a short distance along a path which brought us into a vast court, the farther side of which was scarcely visible. It was entirely covered with matting. Its columns extended in rows, and beside each stood a tall winged chair bound to the column with an iron chain. A turbaned shaikh, like my father, sat in every chair with yellowing pages in his hand, surrounded by circles, straggling or strong, as the case might be, of students, their shoes beside them, dressed in long white, full-sleeved gowns or white galabiyyahs and black clokes, each with the same text-book in his hand as the shaikh, who read aloud and commented while the students listened in silence or engaged in debate.'[1]

So Aḥmad Amīn, reflecting in his autobiography on a first introduction to Al-Azhar in the year AD 1900, just five years before the death of Muḥammad 'Abduh, author of *Risālat al-Tauḥīd*, here presented in English translation, and the most justly celebrated Azhar figure of this twentieth century.

The vast court, with its medley of voices, its forest of columns, and its formidable pundits, so daunting to the shy and tender newcomer not yet in his fourteenth year, is a point of right imaginative departure into the themes and origins of 'Abduh's most representative work. It epitomizes the setting out of which he came and the temper with which he had to contend. Those turbans and text-books and the habits of tradition they represented were the symbol of that *taqlīd*, or bondage to the past,

[1] Aḥmad Amīn: *Ḥayāti*, Cairo, 1950, pp. 50–51.

which was 'Abduh's most persistent object of attack. Yet their wearers and users were the most characteristic exponents of the world to which he belonged and within which his personality was shaped.

Risālat al-Tauḥīd, it is true, was not strictly a document of those precincts. For, as the author's initial narrative indicates, it was composed from notes on lectures he gave in Beirut, Lebanon, during the period when he was in exile from Egypt, following the collapse of the 'Urābī Pasha revolt of 1882. But from 1869 to 1877, 'Abduh had studied in Al-Azhar and in the last decade of the nineteenth century became its vigorous reformer and finally in its closing year the Grand Mufti of Egypt. His teaching, personality and influence constituted the most decisive single factor in the twentieth-century development of Arab Muslim thought and renewal. A vigorous disciple of Jamāl al-Dīn al-Afghānī, the stormy petrel of Islamic revival, whose ardent campaigns first kindled 'Abduh into action, he bequeathed to Muḥammad Rashīd Riḍā, his biographer and founder of the Manār school, an impetus to reform and intellectual initiative which deserved better than in fact it received from the next generation. His tactics were more 'fabian' than those of his great mentor and he relied essentially on educational progress and theological endeavour, corroborated by enlightened legal enterprise. Had he survived to be the 'elder statesman' of the Sa'd Zaghlūl era he might well have returned to the political arena in which he had first tried his wings. For he was gifted with an attractive personality—which the reader must remember, if he cannot always detect, in the more arid portions of the *Risālat*, and it was this which enabled him to sustain his intellectual mission through all the massive inertias of the Azhar mind and to win the title of *Al-Ustādh al-Īmām*, 'the master and guide'.

He owed it in part not only to the tenacity by which he was able to outlive the rigours of his early Azhar days, but also to the Ṣūfī influences of his uncle, Shaikh Darwish, which left their mark in his instinctive piety and his spiritual resilience. Al-Afghānī's activism did the rest, weaning him from possible enervation in mystical asceticism, but without sacrifice of the finer sensitivities that belonged with it. The sense, too, of

Europe, which his travels gave him, and the contacts he enjoyed with French culture, and even in Brighton with Herbert Spencer, saved him from the narrow perspectives of turban and text and their confines of tradition and commentary. If he was eclectic in his reaction to European thought, responding to impulses, whether from Comte or Tolstoi, which he had by no means fully integrated into his ancient loyalties, this was doubtless a hazard of his purpose and is far less reprehensible in his context than its perpetuation in much of the writing and apology that followed in the next two generations. For 'Abduh was essentially a pioneer, initiating what no single generation could hope to complete. Lord Cromer, who was rarely happy in his judgements on Islam, might dub him a 'free thinker' and insist that only in non-reform was Islam itself. The intense opposition which the author of Risālat al-Tauḥīd incurred in many quarters and which asserted itself sharply, as Ṭāhā Ḥusain's autobiography Al-Ayyām relates, after his death, is sufficient proof of his 'modernism'. But if it seems modest in the extreme to a contemporary reader of the work, that will be no more than a vivid measure of the static, indeed, lethargic conservatism against which his efforts were directed. When he died in 1905, through his unfinished Quranic Commentary, his several writings, his legal fatwās and, most of all, by his personal magnetism and integrity of example, he had inaugurated a new temper of religion and scholarship in Egypt to which '. . . more than any other single man (he) gave . . . a centre of gravity and created . . . a literature inspired by definite ideas of progress within an Islamic framework.'[1]

It is this achievement which may be most readily illuminated and assessed from the pages of Risālat al-Tauḥīd, first published in 1897, re-issued with notes and a few significant emendations by Rashīd Riḍā in 1908, and subsequently running through 18 editions up to 1957.

[1] H. A. R. Gibb, in *Bulletin of the School of Oriental Studies*, London, 1928, Vol. iv, p. 758. See the same author's *Modern Trends in Islam*, Chicago, 1946. Also C. C. Adams: *Islam and Modernism in Egypt*, London, 1933, and Albert Hourani: *Arabic Thought in the Liberal Age*, 1798–1939, London, 1962, and *Islam in the West*, ed. R. N. Frye, 'S-Gravenhage, 1957, pp. 149–178, and Kenneth Cragg: *Counsels in Contemporary Islam*, Edinburgh, 1964. These works contain full bibliography on the career of Muḥammad 'Abduh.

Risālat and *Tauḥīd*, as Arabs and Arabists will be quick to insist, are only imperfectly done into English as 'Theology' and 'Unity', though it is hoped by putting these two together as 'The Theology of Unity' no one will be tempted to suppose that this is a treatise about any other kind of unity. To spell this out in 'The Theology of the Divine Unity' seems unnecessary. But it must be remembered that *Tauḥīd* is a causative and intensive noun and never means 'unity', still less 'unitariness', as an abstract state. It is aggressive, so to speak, antiseptic: it means 'unity' intolerant of all pluralism, in the ardent subjugation of all that flouts or doubts it, in the mood so finely captured by Milton in *Samson Agonistes*:

> 'God, nothing more certain, will not long defer
> To vindicate the glory of His Name
> Against all competition, nor will long
> Endure it, doubtful whether God be Lord
> Or Dagon.'

This is the decisive termination of every rivalry of idolatry or defiance which Islamic *Tauḥīd* means, however scholastic the language of its champions or abstruse their rationality. It is for this reason that 'treatise' seems so frail and demure a word and finds no favour here. *Risālat* often requires 'mission' and 'message' hyphened into one (and has on occasions been so translated here). For it means not only what is said but the commission to say it inherent in its nature. This in turn belongs with the urgency of the 'Unity' 'against all competition.' So the definite article is important, too. 'Abduh's book is not about something which is a point of view, a case worth hearing among others. It is positive and assertive because it carries the commission of Islam and serves the apostolate of Muḥammad which is credally one with the Divine unity. What we have to do with here is '*The* Theology of Unity'—assured, militant and crusading.

This is not to say that the author has taken the full measure of his obligations. Indeed, the silences of the book are not the least notable of its features. In the problems of theological language and its meaning and the Names of God, the 'unity' of causation in Divine and human willing, the harmony of revela-

Introduction

tion and reason, and the whole question of 'necessity' in God, 'Abduh is far too readily satisfied with arbitrary 'reconciliations' that leave the essential issue either in ambiguity or pure assertion. The doctrine of the unity, in other words, deserves and demands a much greater thoroughness and far more rigorous standards of intellectual argument than here obtain. Yet, in reviewing these shortcomings for the reader in some detail, it is well to remember that the criteria by which they are found wanting are the highest implicit tribute that could be paid to the intentions and spirit of the *Risālat*.

A start can perhaps be made by noting the manner and substance of his illustrations, the usually concrete realms from which he takes them and an odd unawareness at times of where, if pressed, they might lead him. He is happiest when he is belabouring the obscurantists. Religion with them has become like an old garment which any self-respecting fellow would be embarrassed and ashamed to wear. More oddly, blind readers of the Qur'ān are like donkeys laden with books who have for their pains only a sore back and a loss of breath. Such humour must surely have brought a touch of gaiety to the circle of turbans round the column. But ordinarily 'Abduh does not use the weapon of irony. When he is disdainful he wields a bludgeon rather than a rapier, as when he belabours as perverse and even bestial those who cannot share his confidence about the authenticity of *Waḥy*, or revelation. Here, and elsewhere he is too ready to chastise where he might longer persuade and to castigate where he might further argue. This, too, may be a reflection on his *taqlīd*-bound opponents who could better be cudgelled than convinced.

Writing of the wonder of Quranic eloquence and the negative claim that its being impossible is non-proven, he invokes the analogy of a sick man who is able to survive without food despite his illness, where a healthy man undergoing the same degree of hunger would certainly succumb. The argument is hardly served by the parallel. Disease as a metaphor recurs in the section on the experience of voice and image within prophetic inspiration. If the imaginations of the state of delirium can assume physical actuality for the sufferer, could not the prophet hear and see in a concrete reality? But is the illustration alive to its own implications? Writing again on religion as complementing reason, he comments that animals cannot depend on sight alone but rely on hearing also. He seems unaware of any incongruity in arguing from two physical senses in animals to the vexed and vast issues between the rational and the 'numinous'. Scarcely happier is the illustration that rounds off the answer to the 'ready objection' which follows the exposition of Islam's expansion, that of the doctor who succumbs to the disease he has been treating to such a point that he is incapacitated from taking his own medicine. The idea of contagion and hazard here is, perhaps, right enough. But what is the healing which can be so externalised to itself as to be outside its own range even to preserve, still more to repair? As a parable meant to conclude a case, it is far from reassuring though it is plainly intended so to be. Yet, tested as earlier by its effectiveness for its context, the likeness may be telling enough.

The impression that the reader must keep close to what 'Abduh intended to do and that his immediate effect is surer than his ultimate obligations, is confirmed by his remarks in the discussion of human behaviour, both good and bad. Civil rebellion, he observes, will be concerted by men who are well aware that retribution will be incurred. Yet their knowledge of this by warning does not deter their risky ventures. In other realms, too, knowledge does not decisively shape or control conduct. Why then lay too much stress upon rational persuasion, with all the terminological subtleties it involves? Ordinary people are safe anyway and doctrinaire obscurantists impervious to it. Or at any rate this is so in large measure. So 'Abduh readily breaks off where argumentation becomes too complicated or exacting, confident that this is a truer wisdom both for ordinary mortals and for the incorrigible 'schoolmen'. The long introductory section on the divisions which have brought on the decadence of Islam seems designed to sustain the same point and to illustrate the dangers of intellectual pretension in sectarianism.

Sects, it is true, arise from many more factors than the intellectual. But the argument is clearly a double-edged one. The *Risālat* itself aspires after a careful rationalism which displays

Introduction

itself particularly in the initial discussion of the evidences for the existence of God as the necessary Being. But this has to march with the authenticity of revelation and he is very ready to assume a congruity between what he follows rationally and what he holds religiously. It is, therefore, intriguing to find him reproaching something very similar in the dogmatists of whom he disapproves and who, as he sees them, neglect or evade whatever contravenes their *parti pris*. They believe first, he says, and then prove. 'Rarely does one find among them one who first proves and then believes.' (p. 66) Yet something like this is frequently his own posture. He takes the argument from reason so far, then links on the dogmatic, asserts and sometimes even argues an affinity between the two, but forecloses the matter by warning against over-inquisitiveness, or by alleging obtuseness in his questioners when the affinity is anywhere challenged or suspected. No doubt, against the background of an urgent campaign against *taqlīd* this lack of strict consistency need not be held too rigorously against him. What matters in ambiguous positions is always their intention, and this we may say of 'Abduh was uniformly good.

Yet the dogmatism, whether for reason or with faith, remains. It can be readily illustrated in the familiar theme of the twin sources of theology. Islam is throughout heralded in these pages as the religion of free reason, which is ready to rely on a limited natural theology (exemplified in Chapter 2), and in which men are liberated from the impositions of belief said to characterize other religions. By intelligence men may arrive at the necessity of Almighty Being and may know that He has attributes without attaining to know these as they are. There is nothing in the whole range of Islam which transcends reason's discovery or, where not discovery, recognition, except such meaningless questions as why there are five ritual movements in the *Ṣalāt* at one time of day and three at another, or the stone-throwing pilgrimage. About such ritual things there must be a certain arbitrariness. But for the rest reason is the scrutineer of evidences and the assessor of dogma.

At the same time, however, it is assumed that such rational liberty will always approve what the faith declares. Having, rationally, acknowledged the mission of a prophet reason must go along with all that he says, whether or not it is able to penetrate the mysteries, assured, however, that in this 'docility' it will not be humiliated with irrationalities that contradict its principles, such as the simultaneous assertion of two incompatibles. 'Abduh does not stay to think what may be the situation when the contents of dogma or prophecy set up tensions for the rational mind far subtler than the simple law of contradiction which, as he says, prophecy will never defy. He is aided, in part, in this attitude by his conviction that ordinary people respond readily to truth in religious guise and have only very modest mental ambitions, and by his careful, and interesting, isolation of dogmatic or revealed truth from the business of investigative science (p. 103). The idea that revelation, without being inimical to reason, is for *religious* truth is one which was to recur frequently in the writings of his successors.

There remains, however, in unresolved suspension the ultimate issue about the compatibilities of faith and reason. The assumption of their congruity needs a much fuller and sterner examination than 'Abduh either makes or concedes and the irresolution here became part of his legacy.

It is implicit, too, in the treatment he gives to the question of prophetic status. Here classical apology, whether medieval or modern, has always sought to hold together a belief in the unique endowment and exceptional capacity of prophets and an insistence on their purely human quality. With Muḥammad this issue inevitably becomes paramount. On the one hand there is the 'miracle' of *I'jāz*. The Qur'ān, with its matchless eloquence, its surpassing Arabic quality, reaches men through the instrumentality of an illiterate messenger, who could not possibly have produced it by normal, literary or personal competence. On the contrary, it manifestly derived from beyond him. His simplicity of origin and its inimitable worth alike testified to its Divine source. But on the other hand, Muḥammad, like all other prophets though in superlative degree, is seen as immune from human blemish. Even physical deformity would be unseemly in the prophetic role, for it would breed a disquieted scepticism in the observer. (Is there here some echo of the instinctive Islamic reluctance to hold mission and crucifixion together in any Divine economy?) Much more would ordinari-

Introduction

ness in other spheres fit ill with prophecy, where 'extraordinary status assures the hearers that the prophet speaks from God' (p. 75). So the prophetic souls are brought to excellence, and entrusted not only with their message but with a perfection of nature, a blessedness of spirit, which would mean death to any other mortals (p. 84).

Are we to understand this unique status as a *post facto* exaltation, as the form in which by association men learn to revere and obey with a 'numinous' wonder the content of the delivered message, that prophets are 'hallowed' in these terms by their experience of recipience? Or is the status a prior pledge and condition of the calling? If, as all the indications are, we should believe the second, how does this prior quality of metaphysical excellence co-exist with the steady emphasis on the illiterate, simple, miraculous, even arbitrary, condition in which the revelation comes? Can we, in other words, hold the miracle of eloquence through the unlettered and a perfected immunity from the blemishes of ordinary humanity? Should not such eminence of the 'text' on the one score and eminence of the personality on the other score have some vital interrelation? But if they had, what precisely becomes of the traditional account of the Quranic miracle?

Again, the 'openness' of this question was, perhaps, of no crippling moment in the context of 'Abduh's own *Risālat*. But it remains as a theological question for his readers, and finds incidental echo in his own unresolved dilemma as to whether or not there is prophetic 'blemish' or 'error' outside the state of *Waḥy* (p. 80). It also bears upon a crucial problem of all Quranic exegesis, namely the relation of the context to the commentary. The more firmly we assert the inherent superiority of the messenger over humankind the more we liberate him, at least by implication, from the involvements of time and place and the liabilities of contextual setting. The Qur'ān, as 'Abduh himself requires, is to be interpreted, at least initially, in accordance with the understanding of those among whom it was sent down. It was of course in such local context that the 'miracle' of eloquence was most apposite and relevant, while it becomes almost wholly inoperative in other times and places. But it would seem to be rather the reverse with the 'surpassingness' of

B

the messenger's status, which would come more fully into its own in the long perspectives of history and the world.

This leads again into the possibility of the double meaning of the Quranic text—its immediate sense for a local and contemporary obedience and its esoteric or universal import through the centuries or among the thoughtful. Many apologists, ancient and recent, in Islam have ventured this distinction. It rides with the whole problem of religious language as such. 'Abduh does not treat here the large question about the *Muḥkamāt* and the *Mutashābihāt*, the categorical and the allegorical, in Quranic terminology. Nor, perhaps oddly in view of his concern here for Divine unity, does he discuss the feasibility of the Divine Names, which are so central an element in Islamic theology. For in applying to God terms which necessarily have a genesis of meaning from the human realm, he is involved with all his fellow theologians of the mosque, in the possibility of meaningful theology. This possibility Christian faith has seen, and indeed heralded, in the confidence of the Incarnation. But this is an assurance not open as an option within the terms of Islamic theology, with its unyielding understanding of a transcendance that, despite creation, revelation, law and prayer, which all presuppose the contrary, never takes human relations essentially into itself. *Risālat al-Tauḥīd* does not broach the most pressing and radical obligation of Islamic unity, namely its relation to the understanding of unity upon which Christianity proceeds.

There is one intriguing sideline to this theme in a rather unusual comment about the basic meaning of *Shirk*, or not letting God be God, which is fundamental to all Islamic religion. 'Abduh employs this concept to castigate a refusal to utilise the normal procedures of causation, such as military resources for doing battle and securing conquest, or natural efficiencies in the external order which lead to expected results. For this causation, whether natural or sensible, is part of the constitution of things as God ordered them. To neglect, by-pass, or displace these, for alternative forms of action, is a form of substitution of some other reliance for that which we owe to God in the employment of His duly ordered processes. Such conduct infers that there are other, even superior, causations than those which God has given. So by employing these we exalt what is not

Introduction 19

Divine to a Divine authority: we deliberately wish another dispensation. That to be remiss about military preparedness, or negligent of medicines God has given, is a form of *Shirk* is a fascinating window on *islām* as an approach to existence. But surely the argument requires a greater sophistication than it receives. For taken seriously, it would seem to exclude the sort of 'criticism' of existing 'givens' which has been the cutting edge of scientific and technological development. Or perhaps we should understand him as meaning that it is the situation of mutuality, within science, between the 'givens' of nature and the employments by man, which constitutes the form of *islām* to which we are called. But it is precisely such activity which sharpens the temptations to human omnicompetence and makes the more urgent and critical those deeper submissions of man to the Divine will that we call economic, political, moral and spiritual—all of them vastly more crucial than the rational submissions made by science to the order of nature. About other, and adventurous, understandings of what *Shirk* may be seen to mean, 'Abduh is silent.[1]

All this leads in turn to the vexed yet exhilarating issue of will—human and Divine. *Risālat al-Tauḥīd*, like every sound Islamic text, is sure that there are no necessities in God. We can never attribute 'duty' to God: there is nothing that He 'ought' to do. All the attributes of His acts are affirmed 'by the special option of His power' (p. 57). There is nothing 'good' for the universe which is incumbent upon Him. We cannot think of God as being rightly under criticism for what He does or does not do, or being applauded because He has vindicated an expectation. Yet how much Biblical revelation would be atrophied, or rather stillborn, by this criterion—if Job could not inveigh against omnipotence or Jeremiah complain in bitterness of soul. In this urge to keep the Divine in total non-necessity, 'Abduh shows himself in line with a fundamentally Islamic instinct. He gives it a sober and gentle assertion, leaving to the inscrutable the equation between *that* God wills it and that it is good. But he is as reluctant as any of his fellows in all the centuries to take

---

[1] See, especially, *Qaryah Ẓālimah*, Cairo, 1954, in which Kāmil Ḥusain explores the potential of the *Shirk* concept. (English translation: *City of Wrong*, Amsterdam, 1959.)

the necessity, so to speak, within the being of God and see the Divine nature as properly under the 'ought' which is its own and, therefore, to some degree one that by revelation we can apprehend and expect. Such a readiness in theology opens the door to a far more secure and authentic practice of prayer and adoration. It also revolutionises the understanding of the nature and pattern of revelation.

It is in this context that we may set the perennial debate of Islamic theology about the createdness or otherwise of the Qur'ān itself. From one point of view the Qur'ān, as God's Word, cannot be thought of as 'coming to be'. It must be as eternal as His knowledge and His will. Hence the insistence that it was uncreated and eternal. Yet, in the temporal realm there is clearly an initiative by which it is inaugurated, as a descended Book on 'the night of power'. God, being under no necessity, acts therein spontaneously and within a genuine option. Whatever we may say about the mystery of God's eternal attribute of speech, there is no necessity about the 'incidence' thereof in the Qur'ān of which Muḥammad, thirteen years before the Hijrah, begins to be the recipient. God cannot be held eternally under the obligation of that initiative. From this angle it must be seen to-come-to-be within the freedom of His will, though it is eternally in His knowledge.

The issue, of course, merges into other themes, notably the time-eternity equation. But it is useful to place it squarely within the debate about 'necessity' and God. For if, by help of this controversy, we can appreciate a consistency between the Divine knowledge and the Divine will (since, though its incidence is temporal, the idea of the Qur'ān is not one that 'occurs' to God), we may perhaps begin to glimpse an equation between the Divine nature and the Divine will and, thus, a necessity of essential nature, by which revelation or truth would be not only an affirmative about God but an imperative within Him.

In the realm of human willing, 'Abduh is careful to hold together the 'reconciliation' associated with the idea of *kasb*. Known to God from the beginning are all the ways of men. But this 'actuality' of those choices, as deeds as good as done, does not detract from their being veritably options within men's experience. By the exercise of will they are 'acquired' (hence

Introduction

kasb, or 'acquisition') by the doer, in whose will the will of God is done. If one, suspecting this 'solution', presses the question whether the doer could have avoided the 'acquisition' and, if not, whether the 'option' was not in effect illusory, we begin to reach towards those over rational pretensions, those improper ambitions of curiosity, against which 'Abduh repeatedly warns his readers, as the enemy both of faith and peaceable religion. But he will hasten to add that these admonitions imply or involve no infringement of rational privilege, no impairment of the intellectual stature of believers. There perhaps it is our wisdom, at least here, to leave the problem too. Our purpose is not to penetrate further than the writer whose acquaintance we intend.

It is his merit to have seen and faced the real perversities of human nature and man's capacity for the rejection of the good. There is a reach to human cupidity far beyond the requirements of mere security or ease. Man has indeed a power of self-destruction (though the Quranic *zulm al-nafs*, or self-wronging, is not explored here) which defies both the dictates of law and the ideals of love. Yet, for all his penetration here, it must be doubted whether his confident conclusion in the chapter on 'Man's Need of the Prophetic Mission' is not a relapse into naïveté. A similar suspicion must attach to his optimistic conclusions at the close of the book about man's 'manuduction' into goodness through the final revelation. There is a certain economic 'innocence' in his picture of exhortation neutralising the grudges of the poor by enjoining on the rich a disarming charity. Like the vast majority of his successor apologists in non-Arab as well as Arab Islam, he sadly underestimates the tenacity of economic ills and never raises the fundamental questions of right, privilege and deprivation, nor does he interrogate the whole system within which the rich could fulfil his admonitions and the poor wait wistfully and, as the Marxist would say, endlessly.

This silence is perhaps the more surprising for the general realism of Islam, which 'Abduh shares, about the necessity for 'the sword of peace'. Muslim militancy in the early days is seen, as in most alert apology, to be the inescapable form of religious 'integrity'. A faith's first and paramount duty is to ensure its own survival, since on this depends the whole viability of its mission. There is 'a Divine imperative by which the struggle in the created world between right and wrong, good and evil, is unrelenting, until God gives the verdict' (p. 148). Refusal to join that issue in concrete, physical terms is either a dereliction of duty, or an idle 'pacificism' or 'tolerance' of evil, though in the kindly shape of sorrows and suffering. Both are bootless. It is not by enduring the obstacles, but by removing them, that the will of God is done. Seen by the contrasted Christian assessments, which in *Risālat al-Tauḥīd*, 'Abduh only briefly notices in a historical summary, though he handles some of them elsewhere,[1] there is a strange ambivalence about this activism. For it belongs with a religious ethos which more than any other has insisted that God's will and power have a competence that needs no human intervention to achieve its victories and designs. Yet there is for Islam a proper, indeed a critical, human belligerence *fī sabīl Illāh*, 'in the way of God', and in this way it is inadequate and improper only to suffer in His Name.

In all the foregoing it will be seen that Muḥammad 'Abduh is the unfailing mentor of all subsequent apology. There is hardly a theme, or an instinct, of Islamic self-expression or vindication which does not find anticipation in the pages of *Risālat al-Tauḥīd*. It might equally well be called *Risālat al-Tajdīd*. For it embraces all that Islamic thought has broadly taken to be the shape and argument of its renewal in this century. All the points are here—the bane and blight of *taqlīd*; the ready 'harmony' of faith and reason; the pragmatic vindication of Islamic history; the Divine omnipotence served by human energy; the paradox of the Prophet's illiteracy and surpassing status; the success of primitive Islam; the disservice done by actual Muslims to proper Islam and the call to present discontent in the cause of true renewal. It is the measure of 'Abduh's pioneering genius that these have become the recurrent notes of the six decades since his death. His *Risālat* is, therefore, a work of central importance in the study of the changes and the continuities of mind that belong with Islam as it approaches the close of its fourteenth century.

[1] In *Al-Islām wa-l-Naṣrāniyyah* etc., Cairo, 1902. ('Islam and Christianity, Science and Civilisation.')

Introduction

H. A. R. Gibb once referred to 'present religious attitudes and movements' as 'the most treacherous field of all' in Islamic studies.[1] It is, then, perhaps the more remarkable that a most obvious guide-book should have remained so long without an English translation. To venture one is, by the same token, both a duty and a good intent.

[1] *Modern Trends. op. cit.* p. viii.

KENNETH CRAGG

Contents

FOREWORD	*page*	7
TRANSLATOR'S INTRODUCTION		9

RISĀLAT AL-TAUḤĪD

AUTHOR'S PREFACE		27
1.	PROLEGOMENA	29
2.	THE CATEGORIES OF KNOWLEDGE The Impossible, the Contingent, the Real Existence of the Contingent	41
3.	THE PRINCIPLES OF THE NECESSARILY EXISTING Eternity, Perpetuity, Wholeness, Life, Knowledge, Will, Almightiness and Freedom of Choice, Unity.	45
4.	THE DIVINE ATTRIBUTES	53
5.	THE ACTS OF GOD	57
6.	THE DEEDS OF MAN Good and Evil Deeds	60
7.	THE PROPHET AS THE HELPER	76
8.	MAN'S NEED OF PROPHETIC MISSION	81
9.	THE POSSIBILITY OF REVELATION	94
10.	REVELATION AND MISSION IN THEIR ACTUALITY The Role of the Messengers of God, A Well-known Objection.	99
11.	THE MISSION AND MESSAGE OF MUHAMMAD	109
12.	THE QUR'ĀN	118
13.	THE ISLAMIC RELIGION, OR ISLAM	123

Contents

14. RELIGIONS AND HUMAN PROGRESS: 132
    THEIR CULMINATION IN ISLAM

15. THE EXPANSION OF ISLAM: ITS 142
    UNPARALLELED SPEED

16. A READY OBJECTION 151

17. ACCEPTING THE TRUTH OF MUḤAMMAD'S 155
    MESSAGE

CONCLUSION 159

INDEX 161

RISĀLAT AL-TAUḤID
Author's Preface

'In the Name of the merciful Lord of mercy.'
'Praise be to God, the Lord of the worlds, the merciful Lord of mercy; Lord of the day of judgement. Thee it is we worship; of Thee we seek for aid. Guide us in the path of rectitude, the path of those upon whom Thou art gracious, not the path of those who are under Thy wrath, nor of the erring.'

Following the events of 1299 AH, when I was in Beirut during my exile from Egypt, I was invited, in 1303 AH, to undertake teaching in the Madrasat al-Sulṭāniyyah. Among the subjects was the theology of unity. I became convinced that lectures on this theme fell short of their objective and failed to benefit the students. The major works were beyond their comprehension and the intermediate text-books were in the idiom of another time. I came to the conclusion that it would be more appropriate to present things to them in closer relation to their capacities. So I fitted my various lectures to the different classes concerned. To the first class I lectured in a readily comprehensible style. Where the art of discussion was not familiar I used to start with the making of premises and went through to the conclusions, with no concern other than the validity of the proofs. I did not mind if in the process I diverged from generally accepted arguments. I made only remote allusions to controversial matters, of a kind that possibly only the initiated could have handled.

These lectures, however, survived only in the notebooks of the students. I, for my part, retained nothing of them. Afterwards my way took me back to Egypt and in the providence of God I was taken up with things other than teaching and forgot the lectures. The entire material passed out of my mind until, after a period of months, I formed the idea of resuming these intellectual and spiritual preoccupations and devoting my time to the subject of the Divine unity. For I realized that it belonged with the very structure of serious existence. Recalling my earlier exertions and knowing they held the clue to future hopes in this field, I resolved to write to some of the students with the request that they send me my lecture notes. thus saving me time which I sorely needed, that I would otherwise have expended in putting together again what I was ready to utilise.

I mentioned this to my brother, Ḥammūdah bey 'Abduh, who told me he had copied my lectures as dictated to the introductory class. On securing and reading the text, I found it very much to my liking. While any novice would need the form it took, it seemed calculated also to fit the requirements of the more experienced student. It was a well conceived summary, within deliberate limits. It kept closely to the primitive authorities without impugning their successors' views. And it avoided the disputations of the schools of law with their barren wrangles.

Yet I was aware that in some respects it showed a brevity of treatment which might be less than satisfactory to the student, neglecting matters he needed to know, while in some areas exceeded what should be expected in a summary of this kind.

Accordingly, I simplified certain expressions and elaborated what was abstruse in the argument, adding where there had been negligent omissions and abridging parts that were over-written. In publishing it, my faith was in God that its concise form would not disserve its theme or detract from its effectiveness. It is the human lot humbly to serve and to be served. God alone is the sovereign patron from whom all aid is sought.

Chapter 1

PROLEGOMENA

DEFINITION OF *TAUḤĪD*
THE MEANING AND SOURCE OF THE TERM

The theology of unity (*Tauḥīd*) is the science that studies the being and attributes of God, the essential and the possible affirmations about Him, as well as the negations that are necessary to make relating to Him. It deals also with the apostles and the authenticity of their message and treats of their essential and appropriate qualities and of what is incompatibly associated with them.

The original meaning of *Tauḥīd* is the belief that God is one in inalienable divinity. Thus the whole science of theology is named from the most important of its parts, namely the demonstration of the unity of God in Himself and in the act of creation. From Him alone all being derives and in Him alone every purpose comes to its term. Unity was the great aim of the mission of the Prophet Muḥammad, the blessing and peace of God be upon him. This is entirely evident from the verses of the mighty Qur'ān, as will fully appear below.

The doctrine of unity could equally well be called scholastic theology. One reason for this lies in the fact that the chief point of debate at issue between the learned of the early centuries was whether the Quranic word was created or pre-existent. Another may lie in the fact that theology is built on rational demonstration as alleged by each theologian in his spoken case. For in their rationality they only occasionally appealed to dogmatic tradition (*naql*) and then only after establishing the first principles from which they went on yet again to further deductions, like branches of the same stem. The name may perhaps also be credited to the fact that these scholastic methods of proof in theology were comparable to those of logic in its procedures of argument within the speculative sciences. So *Kalām*, or scholastic theology was used as a term in preference to logic, to denote the distinction between the two, with their identical procedures but differing subject-matter.

This branch of science, dogmatic theology and prophetic interpretation, was known among the nations before Islam. There were in every people custodians of religion concerned with its protection and propagation, of which the first prerequisite is expression. They had, however, little recourse to rational judgement in their custody of belief. They rarely relied for their ideas and dogmas on the nature of existence or the laws of the universe. Indeed there is an almost total contrast between the intellectual cut and thrust of science and the forms of religious persuasion and assurance of heart. Oftentimes religion on the authority of its own leaders was the avowed enemy of reason, and all its works. Theology consisted for the most part of intricate subtleties and credulous admiration of miracles, with free play to the imagination—a situation familiar enough to those acquainted at all with the condition of the world before the coming of Islam.

The Qur'ān came and took religion by a new road, untrodden by the previous Scriptures, a road appropriate and feasible alike to the contemporaries of the revelation and to their successors. The proof of the prophethood of Muḥammad was quite a different matter from that of earlier prophecies. It rested its case on a quality of eloquence, belonging even to the shortest chapter of it, quite beyond the competence of the rhetoricians to reproduce, though in his recipience of the revelation he was simply a man. The Book gives us all that God permits us, or is essential for us, to know about His attributes. But it does not require our acceptance of its contents simply on the ground of its own statement of them. On the contrary, it offers arguments and evidence. It addressed itself to the opposing schools and carried its attacks with spirited substantiation. It spoke to the rational mind and alerted the intelligence. It set out the order in the universe, the principles and certitudes within it, and required a lively scrutiny of them that the mind might thus be

Prolegomena

sure of the validity of its claims and message. Even in relation of the narratives of the past, it proceeded on the conviction that the created order follows invariable laws, as the Qur'ān says: 'Such was the way of God in days gone by and you will find it does not change' (Surah 48,23). And again: 'God does not change a people's case until they change their own disposition' (Surah 13.11). '... the shape of religious man as God has made him. There is no altering the creation of God' (Surah 30.30). Even in the realm of the moral it relies on evidence: 'Requite evil with good and your worst enemy will become your dearest friend' (Surah 41.34). Thus for the first time in a revealed Scripture, reasons finds its brotherly place. So plain is the point that no elucidation is required.

Saving those who give place to neither reason nor faith, all Muslims are of one mind in the conviction that there are many things in religion which can only be believed by the way of reason, such as the knowledge of God's existence, of His power to send messengers, of His knowledge of the content of their inspiration, of His will to give them particular messages, and, with these, many consequent points relating to the comprehension and evidence of prophetic mission. So Muslims are of one mind that though there may be in religion that which transcends the understanding, there is nothing which reason finds impossible.

The Qur'ān describes the attributes of God, by and large, with a far surer accent of transcendance than the earlier religions. Nevertheless, there are several human attributes, which, in name or form, are made comparable, such as power, choice, hearing and seeing. In what is ascribed to God we find points that have counterparts in man, like taking one's seat upon a throne, and like the face and the hands. The Qur'ān deals at length with predestination and human free-will, and takes controversial issue with those who exaggerate on both sides of this theme. It affirms the reward of good deeds and the retribution of evil deeds and leaves the recompense of approbation and punishment to the arbitrament of God. In this introduction there is no need to expatiate further on similar topics.

This Quranic esteem for the rational judgement, together with the use of parables in the allegorical or ambiguous passages in the revealed text, gave great scope to alert intelligences, the more so inasmuch as the appeal of this religion to reason in the study of created things was in no way limited or hedged about with conditions. For it knew that every sound study would conduce to belief in God, as Quranically depicted. So it had no need of either excessive abstraction or over-rigorous definition.

The Prophet's day passed—he who was men's recourse in perplexity and their lamp in the darkness of doubt. His two immediate successors in the Caliphate devoted their span of life to repelling his foes and ensuring the unity of the Muslims. Men had little leisure at that time for critical discussion of the basis of their beliefs. What few differences there were they took to the two Caliphs and the Caliph gave his decision, after consultation, if necessary, with the available men of insight. These issues, for the most part, had to do with branches of law, not with the principles of dogma. Under those two Caliphs, men understood the Book in its meaning and allusions. They believed in the transcendence of God and refrained from debate about the implications of passages involving human comparisons. They did not go beyond what was indicated by the literal meaning of the words.

So the case remained until the events which resulted in the death of the third Caliph—a tragedy which did irreparable damage to the structure of the Caliphate and brutally diverted Islam and the Muslim people from their right and proper course. Only the Qur'ān remained unimpaired in its continuity. As God said: 'It is We who have sent down the Reminder and We truly preserve it' (Surah 15.9). And thus the way was open for man to transgress the proper bounds of religion. The Caliph had been killed with no legal judgement and thus the popular mind was made to feel there could be free rein to passion in the thoughts of those who had not truly allowed the faith to rule in their hearts. Lawless anger had possessed many of the very exponents of pious religion. Both worldlings and zealots together had overborne the steadfast people and set in motion a train of consequences they could only deplore.

Among the actors in that crisis of disloyalty was 'Abdallāh ibn Saba', a Jew whom had embraced Islam and an excessive admirer of 'Alī (whose face God honour) to the point of asserting

Prolegomena

that God indwelt him. Ibn Saba' claimed that 'Alī was the rightful Caliph and rebelled against 'Uthmān who exiled him. He went to Basrah where he propagated his seditious views. Evicted from there, he went to Kūfā, taking his poison with him, and thence to Damascus, where he failed to find the support he wanted. He proceeded to Egypt where he did find collaborators with the dire consequences we know. In the time of 'Alī, when his school showed its head again, he was exiled to Madā'in. His ideas spawned a lot of later heresies.

Events took their subsequent course. Some of those who had pledged allegiance to the fourth Caliph broke their fealty. Civil war ensued, issuing in the hegemony of the Umayyads. But the community had been sundered and its bonds of unity broken. Rival schools of thought about the Caliphate developed and were propagated in partisanship, each striving by word and act to gain the better over its adversary. This in turn gave rise to forgeries of traditions and interpretation, and the sectarian excess brought sharp divisions into Khawārij, Shī'ah and moderates. The Khawārij went so far as to declare their opponents infidels and to demand a republican form of government. For a long time they maintained their 'excommuncation' of those who resisted them, until after much fighting that cost many Muslim lives their cause grew weak. They fled into remoter parts but continued their seditious activities. A remnant of them survives to the present in certain areas of Africa and of the Arabian peninsula. The Shī'ahs carried their heresy to the point of exalting 'Alī or some of his descendants to Divine or near-Divine status, with widespread consequences in the field of dogma.

These developments, however, did not halt the propagation of Islam and did not deprive the areas remote from the centre of controversy of the light of the Qur'ān. People came into Islam in droves—Persians, Syrians and their neighbours, Egyptians and Africans, and others in their train. Freed from the necessity of defending the temporal power of Islam, great numbers were ready to busy themselves with the first principles of belief and law, in pursuance of the Qur'ān's guidance. In this task, they gave due place to the delivered tradition without neglecting the proud role of reason or overlooking the intellect. Men of sincere integrity took to the vocation of knowledge and education, the most famous of them being Ḥasan al-Baṣrī. He had a school in Basrah to which students came from every part and various questions were examined. People of all religious persuasions had come into Islam without knowing it inwardly, but carrying with them into it their existing notions, seeking some kind of mediating compromise between the old and the Islamic. So after the tempests of sedition came the tensions of doubt. Every opinion-monger took his stand upon the liberty of thought the Qur'ān enjoined. The newcomers asserted their right to an equal stake with the existing authorities, and schisms raised their heads among the Muslims.

The first theme of contention to arise was that of will—man's independence in willing and doing and choosing, and the question of the supreme sin unrepented of. Wāṣil ibn 'Aṭā' and his master, Ḥasan al-Baṣrī, differed on this issue and the former broke away, teaching according to his own independent lights. Many of the first Muslim masters, including Ḥasan al-Baṣrī, or so it is alleged, were of the view that man truly has choice in the deeds which proceed from his knowledge and will. So they opposed the school of *Jabr*, or determinism, which held that man in his volitional activity is like the branches of a tree swaying necessarily. Throughout the period of the rule of Marwān's sons no effort was made to regulate the issue or to get people back to first principles and bring them to a common position. Individual idiosyncrasy had free play, though 'Umar ibn 'Abd al-'Azīz gave directions to Al-Zahrā to record the traditions he had come by and he was the first tradition-collector.

These two problems, however, were not all. Controversy developed also over the question whether the real attributes of God should be posited of the Divine essence or not. There was also the question of reason and its competence to know all religious principles, even the ramifications of law and matters pertaining to worship, which some espoused even to the point of excessive pleading of the Quranic text. Others limited the writ of reason to the first principles, as explained above. Others again—a minority—in a spirit of contention against the first group, totally repudiated reason and thus went counter to the

Prolegomena 35

Qur'ān itself. Opinions on the Caliphs and the Caliphate marched with those on matters of doctrine, as if they were an integral part of Islamic dogma.

With the disciples of Wāṣil the paths diverged further. For they had recourse to drawing congenial ideas from the Greeks. They had the idea that it was a work of piety to establish dogma by scientific corroboration, without discriminating, however, between what went back to rational first principles and what was merely a figment of the imagination. So they mingled with the tenets of religion what had no valid rational applicability. They persisted on this tack until their sects multiplied apace. The 'Abbāsid rule, then in the prime of power, helped them and their views prevailed. Their learned scholars began to write books. Whereupon the adherents of the schools of the early masters took up their challenge, sustained by the power of conviction though lacking the support of the rulers.

The early 'Abbāsids knew the extent of their debt to the Persians for the successful establishment of their power and the overthrow of the Umayyad state. They relied strongly on Persian collaboration and brought them into high positions among their ministers and retainers. Many of them thus came into authority without any part or lot in Islam religiously, including Manichee sectaries and Yazidīs, and other Persian persuasions, as well as utterly irreligious people. They began to disseminate their opinions and by attitude and utterance induced those to whom their views were congenial to accept their direction. Atheism emerged, and views inimical to belief in God became rife, to the point that Al-Manṣūr ordered the issue of books exposing their errors and negating their claims.

At this juncture the science of theology was still a young plant, a still partly reared edifice. Technical theology took its point of departure from its perpetual principle, namely the study of the created order, within the terms laid down by the Qur'ān. There ensued here the dispute over the createdness or uncreatedness of the Qur'ān. Several of the 'Abbāsid Caliphs adopted the dogma of the Qur'ān's being created, while a considerable number of those who held to the plain sense of the Qur'ān and the Sunnah either abstained from declaring themselves or took a stand for uncreatedness. The reticence arose from a reluctance to give expression to what might conduce to heresy. The dispute brought much humiliation to men of reason and piety and much blood was criminally shed. In the name of faith the community did violence to faith.

It was in this way that the lines were drawn between the thoroughgoing rationalists and the moderate or extreme upholders of the text of the law. All were agreed that religious principles were a matter of obligation for their followers, both in respect of acts of worship and mutual dealings, and should be stringently followed. It was recognised that the inner attitudes of heart and the spiritual life constituted a binding obligation to which the soul must be set.

A further element in the picture was the sect of the *Dahriyyūn*, who believed in *ḥulūl* and sought to foist upon the Qur'ān the notions they brought with them on assuming the externals of Islam. They strayed far in their exegesis and pretended to find in every plain deed some hidden mystery. In their handling of the Qur'ān they were as far from the import of the text as error is from truth. They were known as the *Bāṭiniyyah* and the *Ismā'īliyyah*, as well as by other names current among historians. Their schools of thought had a disastrous influence on the faith and undermined conviction. Their deviations and deeds are only too familiar.

Despite the identity of purpose shared by the orthodox and those at issue with them, as to the combating of these atheist sectarians, there were considerable areas of contention between them and the vicissitudes were prolonged. This did not prevent them, however, from mutual borrowing, each group profiting from the other, until the emergence of Shaikh Abū-l-Ḥasan al-Ash'arī early in the fourth century (AH). He plotted a middle course, as is well known, between the early 'orthodox' and the subsequent tendencies towards extremes. He based dogma on the principles of rational enquiry. The disciples of pristine loyalties doubted his views and many maligned him. The followers of Ibn Hanbal called him an infidel and demanded his death. A number of eminent 'ulamā', however, came to his support, among them Abū Bakr al-Bāqillānī, the Imām al-Ḥaramain (Abū-l-Ma'ālī al-Juwaynī) and Al-Isfirā'īnī. His school came to carry the name of *Ahl al-Sunnah wa-l-Jamā'ah*.

Prolegomena

Two powerful forces were effectively overcome by these esteemed thinkers—the temper that leans wholly on the literal and the instinct that runs off into the imaginary and the extravagant. Two centuries or so later these types survived only as insignificant pockets of opinion in the periphery of the Islamic world.

The disciples of Al-Ash'arī's school, it should be remembered, having based their doctrine rationally on the laws of the universe, required the believer as a matter of obligation to hold the certainty of these rational premises and deductions in the same assurance with which he accepted the dogmas of faith, insisting that where proof was wanting the to-be-proven was non-existent also. That outlook continued until the rise of Al-Ghazālī and Al-Rāzī and those who adopted their position, according to whom one or even several proofs could be shown to be false and yet leave open the possibility of the object whose existence it was intended to demonstrate being substantiated from more adequate evidence. There was, they held, no justification for making the argument from the negative instance absolute.

As for the schools of philosophy, they drew their ideas from pure reason and the only concern of philosophic rationalists was to gain knowledge, to satisfy their intellectual curiosity in elucidating the unknown and fathoming the intelligible. They were well able to achieve their objectives, inasmuch as they were sheltered by the mass of religious believers who afforded them full liberty of action to enjoy and give rein to their intellectual interests, the pursuit of crafts and the strengthening of of the social order through the disclosure of the secrets hidden in the universe—all in accordance with the Divine mandate for such exploration by thought and mind: 'He created for you all that is in the earth' (Surah 2.29), which exempts neither the seen nor the unseen. Not a single intelligent Muslim sought to debar them or to impede their findings, the Qur'ān having espoused the high role of reason and confirmed its competence as the ultimate means to happiness and the criterion between truth and falsehood, worth and loss. Had not the Prophet observed: 'You are most cognizant of the world and its ways,' and given at the battle of Badr an example of behaviour based on intelligent discernment and the proof of experience?

Nevertheless, it is clear that most of the philosophers were subject to two influences that got the better of them. The first was an admiration for all that derived from the Greek philosophers, notably Plato and Aristotle, and with it a too precipitate inclination to accept their authority. Secondly, there was the prevailing contemporary trend of will, and this had the more mischievous effects. For they got themselves into controversies obtaining among speculative thinkers in the field of religion. Though there were relatively few of them, they clashed with the beliefs predominantly held, and so came under attack. Then came Al-Ghazālī and his school and brought sharp criticism to bear upon the entire content of philosophical lore in the fields of theology and related themes, including the principles of substance and accident, theories of matter and physics and, indeed, the whole gamut of rationality in relation to religion. Later exponents of this criticism became so extreme as to forfeit their following. Ordinary people turned from them and the specialists became indifferent to them. In due course, time precluded the results the Muslim world might have expected from their activities.

All this explains why matters of theology mingle with philosophy in the writings of later authors like Al-Baiḍāwī, Al-'Aḍad and others, and why various rational sciences became concentrated in a single pursuit, the assumptions and debates of which approximated more to a traditionalism than a rationalism, whereby the progress of knowledge was arrested.

Then there supervened the various successive insurrections aimed at the civil power, in which it was the obscurantists who got the upper hand, destroying the remaining traces of the rational temper which had its source in the Islamic faith. They betook themselves to devious by-paths and students of the writings of the previous generations found themselves limited to mere wrangles about words and scrutiny of methods—and that in a very few books characterised by feebleness and mediocrity.

As a consequence a complete intellectual confusion beset the Muslims under their ignorant rulers. Ideas which had never had any place in science found sponsors who asserted things Islam had never before tolerated. Fostered by the general

Prolegomena 39

educational poverty, they gained ground, aided too by the remoteness of men from the pristine sources of the faith. They evicted intellect from its rightful place and dealt arbitrarily with the false and the valid in thinking. They went so far as to espouse the view of some in other nations who alleged an enmity between knowledge and faith. They took up highly misleading positions on questions of both morals and doctrine, things allowed and things forbidden, that is, and even the issues of Islam and the very denial of God. Their fantasies fell very far short of the real meaning of religion while their ideas and language sadly misrepresented God. There can be no doubt that the consequences befalling the masses of men in their beliefs and principles, from this prolonged disaster with its widespread confusion, were grievous and heavy.

The foregoing is a summary of the history of theology, indicating how it was founded on the Qur'ān and how at length partisanship sadly distorted its true goal and quality.

We must, however, believe that the Islamic religion is a religion of unity throughout. It is not a religion of conflicting principles but is built squarely on reason, while Divine revelation is its surest pillar. Whatever is other than these must be understood as contentious and inspired by Satan or political passions. The Qur'ān has cognisance of every man's deed and judges the true and the false.

The purpose of this discipline, theology, is the realisation of an obligation about which there is no dispute, namely, to know God most high in His attributes that are necessarily to be predicated of Him and to know His exaltation above all improper and impossible attribution. It is, with Him, to acknowledge His messengers with full assurance and heart-confidence, relying therein upon proof and not taking things merely upon tradition. So the Qur'ān directs us, enjoining rational procedure and intellectual enquiry into the manifestations of the universe, and, as far as may be, into its particulars, so as to come by certainty in respect of the things to which it guides. It forbids us to be slavishly credulous and for our stimulus points the moral of peoples who simply followed their fathers with complacent satisfaction and were finally involved in an utter collapse of their beliefs and their own disappearance as a community. Well is it said that traditionalism can have evil consequences as well as good and may occasion loss as well as conduce to gain. It is a deceptive thing, and though it may be pardoned in an animal is scarcely seemly in man.

Chapter 2

THE CATEGORIES OF KNOWLEDGE

The objects of our knowing are divided into three categories: that which is contingent, that which is necessarily self-existent and that which is inherently impossible of existence. We name the third that which of itself is non-existent: the necessarily self-existing that which is of itself: the contingent that which does not exist of itself but which exists, or not, according to the presence or absence of that which gives it existence, and becomes necessary or possible by an external other. The notion of that the existence of which is impossible is of course a figurative thing, for if anything is to be thought of as a true object of knowledge it must really exist so that the concept of it can be formed. The essentially non-existent is clearly not thus. Nevertheless, the concept of it is argumentatively necessary as an act of imagination.

THE PRINCIPLE OF THE IMPOSSIBLE

The inherently impossible of existence is that whose existence is inconceivable. Non-existence is inseparable from the very nature of its case. If existence were to be postulated of it, its very essence would be negated; it would, so to speak, be self-falsified. The impossible of existence has no being: it is absolutely and necessarily non-existent. The mind can formulate no existent image for it, as we have said. It therefore does not exist, either in fact or in thought.

THE PRINCIPLES OF THE CONTINGENT

The principle of the contingent is that it is neither existent nor non-existent except by some external cause, since neither of these alternatives is inherent in it and either is equally possible.

If either were to be asserted of it without such cause this would mean the superiority of one of two equals over the other, which is manifestly impossible.

Another principle of the contingent is that when it exists it does so as an 'accident'. For it has been established that it only exists by prior cause. To say, therefore, that it exists prior to the existence of its cause is obviously false. For otherwise the dependent would be preceding that on which it depends, which is contrary to the whole notion of dependence. This has already been shown and is excluded *ex hypothesi*. But if we say, secondly, that the contingent comes into being simultaneously with its cause, this is likewise impossible. For then the two would be equally existent and the question of which was cause and which effect would be open. And this mind cannot brook, inasmuch as there is no reason whereby the cause and effect can be identified. The third, and only, alternative is that the contingent comes into being after the cause: its cause is in existence before it and since the existence of every dependent thing is preceded by its non-existence, every contingent must be said to be so 'dependent' or created.

In its non-existence, the contingent has no need of an existent cause. For non-existence is negative and a negative has no need of becoming existent. So the contingent can be non-existent, either for lack of causation unto it, or for lack of continuance of what caused it. For existence, it necessarily has need of a cause, since nothing cannot be the origin of existence. The existent, if dependent, or created, must be brought into being by a creation. This is entirely evident.

Just as the contingent needs a cause to originate its existence, so it needs a cause for its continuance in being. We have shown that the contingent is not of necessary or self-existence and that it only comes into existence by an external or anterior cause. Therein is a state which may be said to be inherent in the contingent and always attaching to it. The contingent can never be in a state of necessary self-existence: in all circumstances it remains in need of that which gives it being out of non-existence, and this is true both of genesis and perpetuation.

'Cause' in the foregoing means that which creates and gives existence. It may also be described as the originator, the original

The Categories of Knowledge

cause, the operative cause, the real efficient cause, and other such expressions of different construction but roughly identical meaning. Sometimes the cause is so named for the reason that by it as a state or condition the contingent comes to exist, being necessary to the genesis of the contingent though the latter has no need of it for continuance. It may be that the cause will need to be present and then need to be absent, as for example, the builder who is a necessary agent to the coming to be of a house, but can yet die and the house abide. The builder is not the bestower of existence upon the house, though his handiwork, his mental activity and the exercise of his will are all a necessary condition for the existence of the house and its particular form.

In sum, then, there is a difference between the contingent's general dependence on conditions and its actual derivation of existence from something. Its dependence may be on something which is and then ceases to be. The second step in walking, for example, depends upon the first, but the first does not bestow existence on the second. For then it would be imperative that it co-exist with it. The fact, of course, is that the second does not not come into being until the first had passed away, whereas derivation of existence must be from something which antecedently has existence and gives it to the 'receiver' or 'deriver', so that the existence of the latter turns on the existence of the former and cannot be without it, independently, in any of its states.

THE REAL EXISTENCE OF THE CONTINGENT

We see things in existence which earlier did not exist, and others which cease after having been: trees, plants and animals, for example. These 'existers' might theoretically be classified as impossible, necessary or contingent. The first, however, must be ruled out since the impossible of existence never exists. The second must also be excluded, since the necessarily existent is not contingent, does not pass, and non-existence cannot be asserted of it, and has never been true of it, as will appear below, when we deal with the necessarily existing. So then the third alternative is the right one. The things referred to are contingently and emphatically existent.

(The existence of the contingent requires the necessarily existing.)

It is clear that all contingents in existence taken together constitute a contingent. And all contingence needs a cause to give it being. Thus the collectivity of contingents in turn requires a creator or originating cause. It is impossible that this should be the sum of the contingencies, since that would involve a thing being antecedent to itself. And it is impossible that the creator should be part of the collectivity, since this would be to constitute a thing its own cause and cause of all that preceded it (if the creating part were not the first and of itself if it were). Both these suggestions are plainly absurd. Clearly the whole range of contingents must have a cause prior to it and the only non-contingent cause is the necessarily existing. For there is nothing prior to the contingent save the impossible and the necessary. The former has no existence. Therefore there remains only the necessary. So it is proved that the contingents that are have a cause of existence that must necessarily exist.

Furthermore, the contingents that exist do so equally whether they be finite or infinite. If we were to say that this existence had its source within itself, or in the modes of the contingents, it would be untenable, on the ground of what has already been shown in respect of contingents, namely that no mode of the contingents is outside them. It is in the necessarily existing.

Chapter 3

THE PRINCIPLES OF THE NECESSARILY EXISTING

ETERNITY, PERPETUITY AND WHOLENESS

Eternity in the past is one of the properties of the necessary Being. Were it not so there would be a coming-to-be, a creation which before existence was non-existent. Everything preceded by no existence needs a cause to give it being, if we are not to incur the impossibility of postulating the priority of the subsequent. If the necessary being were not eternal its existing would need some other source than itself. But we have already shown that if the necessary is not self-existent it does not correspond to its own proper definition—which is contradictory and impossible. The necessary being, further, can never not be, for to think otherwise would be the negation of the thing, by itself, in the denial of the essential definition, which is a manifest absurdity.

The necessary being, further again, has an essential simplicity. It is non-composite. For were it not so, the constituent elements in its complexity must each pre-exist the whole which is the essence. Each of the parts is other than the essence necessarily. As we have already said, the necessary is that which is self evident, which could not be the case were we to have the whole depend upon something other than itself. If it then were to be held composite the principle of its existence would be made to turn upon the existence of its parts, whereas we have said that it is self-existent by definition. It would be unwarrantable (as a theory of compositeness would require) to admit necessity to the whole without doing so for the parts: rather these would merit it more than the whole, being prior to it. So then the necessary being cannot be involved in compositeness, and this law goes for that being as a mental reality and as an actual reality. The mind cannot conceive the necessary being as having complexity, for then the mentally imagined parts would need some force to eliminate them in the actual or external reality, since otherwise compositeness in the 'idea' would have been reproduced in the real. Our 'idea' and its content would then be a deception and not the reality.

And with the non-compositeness of the necessary being goes its indivisibility into any of the three dimensions. It has no 'extension'. Were it divisible, it would be sustaining something other than its original existence and a multiple existence in the diversified existents into which it was divided. By this means, it would be susceptible either of non-existence or complexity, both of which, as we have said, are impossible to it.

LIFE

The concept of existence, though rationally evident, is mentally 'pictured' from what appears. Its abidingness and constancy follow. There is clearly a relation between the perfection and intensity of existence and the perfection and intensity of the concept.

Each category of existence necessarily entails the most perfect form of the attributes pertaining to that category, as already mentioned. For otherwise the existent would belong to a category other than that which was being asserted of it.

The forms of existence which the soul 'pictures' or conceives are innumerable. The most perfect form in any instance is that which is most ordered and integral and free from faults and confusion. If, so concordant, the form maintains a continuous existence in self-consistency, it is thereby provenly the perfect existent form of that to which the 'picture' relates.

If the soul has 'pictured' to it a category of existence from whence originates all harmony that would indicate therein the most perfect and exalted and intense of all categories.

The existence of the necessary being is the source whence every contingent has existence, as we have said and entirely proved. By the same token, it is the most intense and supreme

The Principles of the Necessarily Existing

of existents. And it is likewise characterised by the attributes appropriate to that supreme quality. The utmost perfection of existence the mind can imagine, in the context of the concepts of abidingness and constancy and manifestation, must be attributed to it, as possible of it. As we have mentioned, the necessary being is the source of all harmony and the control of the natural order in undisturbed continuity and this fact must be reckoned within the perfection of existence and so affirmed. The necessarily existing possesses all the attributes which can be attributed to that category of being.

Among these essential attributes is that of life—an attribute which embraces also knowledge and will. Manifestly, life is indispensable to perfectness of being. Life with all its corollaries is the origin of order, and the law of wisdom. In each of its categories life is the principle by which its manifestation occurs and persists. It is a perfection of existence and may, therefore, be postulated of the necessarily existing, since all such possible perfections must be attributed to it. The necessarily existent is then alive, though with a life different from that of the contingents. The necessarily perfect being is the source of knowledge and will. For otherwise the very contingents would be possessed of something more perfect, whereas we have earlier said that the necessary being is the most supreme and perfect of existents.

Thus the necessary being is the bestower of existence and all that goes therewith. How if it were lacking life could it bestow life? It possesses life then and is the source thereof.

KNOWLEDGE

The attribute of knowledge must be His. What is intended in ascribing the attribute of knowledge is the innate capacity of active awareness. Knowledge is among the things necessary to perfection of existence so it may be considered an attribute of the necessary Being. Since all conceivable perfection must be so ascribed, the necessary Being knows.

It is also clear that knowledge is a perfection also in the contingents and among them are those endowed with it. Were the necessary Being to be denied knowledge, the contingents would be more perfect—manifest absurdity. Indeed, He is the bestower of knowledge in the contingent knower. It is inconceivable that the bestower of knowledge should Himself lack it.

Knowledge in the necessary Being is a necessity of His existence and it is much a higher knowledge as His very being is higher. A more exalted knowledge than His cannot be imagined, for it embraces all that can be known. Otherwise the mind could imagine a more inclusive knowledge belonging to something more perfect than He—which cannot be.

The necessary Being is completely self-subsistent and self-abiding. His knowledge goes with His existence and depends upon nothing external to Himself and is from eternity unto eternity, transcending the means and cogitations of thought and acts of observation. It is necessarily other than the knowledge contingents possess.

What the contingencies comprehend accords with the capacities of awareness that belong with their knowing. Otherwise there is no knowledge.

Among the proofs of knowledge in the necessary Being is what we may observe of the principles and certainties in the order of the contingent universe, and the fact that everything has its place, and each has at hand what is needful for it to be and continue to be. This situation manifests itself readily in the spectacle of things visible, both small and great, high and low. Take the situation among the stars and their dependable interrelation, the fixed law of their movement by which they keep their appointed courses and every star knows its orbit. Were they irregular, the planetary order—indeed the whole universe—would be thrown into confusion. There are other like points which the astronomical sciences expound. All this bears witness to the maker's knowledge and wisdom.

Take, again, what is observable in the detailed study of plants and animals and the powers with which they are endowed, and the organs as needful for the maintenance of life, with faculties and limbs rightly located in their bodies. The insensible things among them, like plants, have a natural capacity to obtain the appropriate food and leave the inappropriate. The seed of the colocynth is there side by side with the melon seed, in one ground and water and in the same cultivation. Yet the one takes

The Principles of the Necessarily Existing 49

from the one context what yields the bitterest poison and the other the most delightful sweetness. Consider too the guidance of the creatures of sense in the employment of their members and organs, and the exercise of all their powers in their proper capacities. It is He who knows the embryo when it is no more than a sperm drop. He knows how, when it is perfected into a creature and has from Him the 'fiat' of independent life, it needs hands, feet, eyes, nose and ears and other, inner, faculties to use in pursuance of its being and in self-protection, as well as the necessity of stomach, liver and lung and the rest of the organs indispensable to growth and life throughout the allotted span.

He knows, for example, the condition of the young pup in the dog world, how when she grows she will bear many litters and so she has many suckling points. One cannot enumerate all the instances of this kind. There are many expositions in the books of botany and biology and in the sciences of natural history, anatomy, medicine and the rest. Researches in all these fields are, however, really only just beginning, despite the volume of unstinted effort and devotion already expended on unveiling the secrets of nature.

Does not this created world, which men of intelligence fall over themselves to investigate until they attain its secrets, in truth bear witness to its originator, the all-knowing, who has given being to every created thing and guided it? Is it possible that nothing but coincidence, the thing we call 'chance', gave rise to all this order? Has chance laid down the laws upon which are built the universes mighty and lowly? Never. The artificer of all is He whom 'not an atom's weight in heaven and earth escapes'. He hears and knows all.

WILL

Will, also, is necessarily an attribute of the self-existent. This is the quality by which the knower chooses among the possibilities before him.

After we have affirmed that He who grants being to contingents is necessarily existing and knowing, and that every actual contingent exists only by His knowledge, it is necessarily also affirmed that He wills. He acts conformably with His knowledge. Every existent has a particular 'destiny' or decree, nature and appointed quality, in limited time and place. These are the 'particularities' proper to it from among the possible forms there are. The particularizing is according to the knowledge of the necessary Being and there is no meaning to 'will' other than this.

However, the common idea of will is that it is the faculty by which a doer approves the doing of his purpose and refrains from the doing. But this meaning cannot be applied to the necessary Being. For it relates to stresses of the creaturely and to purposes that are liable to be frustrated in consequence of the imperfection of knowledge. 'Will' here changes with the judgement and the doer is caught irresolutely between the pros and the cons that press on him.

ALMIGHTINESS

Omnipotence is another necessary quality of the self-existent—the power, that is, of bringing into being and annihilating. Just as the necessary Being knows and wills the origination of the created beings, undoubtedly He has the ability to actualise His will. The doing, by the knower and the willer, of His knowledge and will proceeds by a power to action which He possesses. It is this power or authority to which, alone, omnipotence refers.

FREEDOM OF CHOICE

To affirm these three attributes of knowledge, will and power is, of necessity, to postulate freedom. The sole meaning of this word is the giving effect by power through knowledge to the decision of the will. He is the choosing doer. None of His doings, none of His creative activities, proceed from Him by instigating cause and entailing within existence without His awareness and will. It is not that anything good for the universe is incumbent on Him to take account of because, if He does not do so, He will incur criticism, and so He comes through with it in order to avoid reproach. God is indeed exalted far above all that. The order of the universe and its vast well-being were determined for it by decree of Him who is necessarily Himself, the most perfect and exalted Being. It is the maker's perfection which is reflected in the perfection of the universe. The excellence of the creation is the revelation of the exaltedness of the creator. This surpassing realm of existence in its utmost order depends on inclusive knowledge and absolute will. It derived, and still derives, its being in this surpassing shape: 'Do you think that We have created you in vain and that you do not return unto Us?' (Surah 23.115). This is the meaning of the dictum which declares that His actions are not motivated by objectives, but yet they are far from vain and pointless. It is impossible they should be innocent of wisdom, even if that wisdom in part is hidden from our view.

UNITY

The necessary Being is One, in His essence, His attributes, His existence and His acts. His essential Unity we have established in the foregoing denial of compositeness in Him, whether in reality or conceptually. That He is unique in His attributes means that no existent is equal to Him therein. We earlier showed that attributes correspond to the category of existence and no other existents are comparable to the necessarily existing. Neither do they equal Him in the attributes which belong with existence. By His unity of existence and action we mean His uniqueness in necessity of being and in His consequent giving of being to contingents. This is incontrovertible. For if there were a number of necessarily existing beings, each of them would have definition differing from the others, for otherwise there would be no meaning to multiplicity. With this divergence would go a distinction of attributes, postulated of the several distinctive entities. For it is clear that attributes differ from each other within the difference of the essences to which they belong. Thus the knowledge and the will of the several necessary beings would differ, each in relation to the difference between the beings possessing them, each distinguished from the other.

And these disparities would have the nature of necessity, since the knowledge and will of the necessarily existing derive from the essence inseparably, and not from any external factor. And as has been said, there is no way to change or flux in them.

Likewise we have earlier said that the acts of the necessarily existent derive from it according to knowledge and the decision of will. Then, if multiplicity be hypothecated, the action of each proceeds from a decision differently, essentially, from that of the others. Actions would then differ with the difference in the knowledge and will involved, and would differ irreconcilably. Each, by virtue of its necessary existence and the related attributes, would have the power to bring into existence a plethora of contingents, in each case determining the contingents according to its knowledge and will. There would be no reason why any of these powers should be exercised to the exclusion of another. Their acts would be in conflict with the conflict in their knowing and their willing, and disorder would overtake the order of the universe. Indeed, order would become impossible and the very contingents would cease existence. For the existence of every contingent would inevitably turn upon conflicting knowing and willing, and any one contingent thing would have conflicting existences, which is impossible. 'Were there in the heavens or on earth any other god than God, the heavens and the earth would have gone down in ruin' (Surah 21.22). But their ruin is plainly ruled out. So God most high in essence and attributes is One: His existence and His acts are inalienably His own, and His alone.

Chapter 4

THE DIVINE ATTRIBUTES

The Divine attributes which are to be believed of the necessary Being are thus fully established by rational proof in the foregoing. The sacred law of Islam, and earlier holy laws, corroborated them in the mission and preaching of the Prophet Muḥammad and the preceding prophets.

Among the attributes of which the law tells are those which reason, though able to hold them compatible with the necessary Being, cannot of itself guide us to their recognition. We must acknowledge these attributes to be God's, in obedience to the content of the law and in acceptance of its message as true.

Among these is the attribute of speech. It is written that God spoke to some of the prophets. The Qur'ān speaks of itself as the speech of God. The source of this speech to which man hearkens from God most high is undoubtedly eternally of His essence.

Revelation also affirms the attribute of sight, that is, the faculty of visual awareness, and the attribute of hearing, the power of aural awareness. For, as the Qur'ān has it 'He is the hearer, the seer.' But we must believe that His awareness is not by any instrument, or outward sense, or by the pupil of an eye, or any seeing sense such as we possess.

THE ATTRIBUTES IN GENERAL

A tradition at the outset, to open up this theme. Though it may be unsound it is sustained in its import by the entire Qur'ān. It runs: 'Ponder the creation of God, but do not take your meditations into the Divine essence, or you will perish.'

Any right estimate of human reason will agree that the utmost extent of its competence is to bring us to the knowledge of the accidents of the existents that fall within the range of human conception, either by senses, or feeling or intellection, and then from that to the knowledge of their causation and to a classification of their varieties so as to understand some of the principles appertaining to them. But reason quite lacks the competence to penetrate to the essence of things. For the attempt to discern the nature of things, which necessarily belongs with their essential complexity, would have to lead to the pure essence and to this, necessarily, there is no rational access. So the utmost that our rationality can attain is a knowledge of accidents and effects.

Take, for example, light—the most clear and evident of things. Students have propounded many laws about it and arranged them in a special science. But none of them can understand what it is or penetrate the nature of illumination. They know only about light what every non-student using his eyes knows equally well. And so it goes.

God did not make man with a need to know the essence of things. His need is to know the accidents and the particular qualities. The mark of a sound mind is its satisfaction with ascertaining the relation of these particular qualities to the entities concerned and with conceiving the principles that undergird these relationships. But to occupy oneself with substance is to waste time and expend energy on an impossible goal.

Man is taken up with coming to know the object nearest to him, which is himself. He has sought to know some of the qualities of the soul. Is it accident or essence? Does it precede or is it subsequent to the body? Is it inherent in the body or self-existent and independent? The mind in fact quite fails to come by any agreed answers. The sum of his efforts is the conclusion that man exists, a living being, with feeling and will. All the other relevant facts established about him are derived from these accidents, attainable by external observation. But the essence of man, and even how he is characterized by some of his attributes, these are unknown to him and will remain inaccessible to knowledge.

This is the condition of the human mind in respect of what is equal with, or lower than, itself in existence, and in respect of the deeds he believes issue from him—thought and its correla-

The Divine Attributes 55

tive, movement, and speech. How much more then is it unable for the understanding of the supreme existence? To turn to the transcendant Being, the ever-eternal, is to be aware not merely of a puzzled wonder but a complete incapacity and otherness.

The study of the creation is necessarily salutary in a practical way and lightens for the soul the way to the knowledge of Him whose are these traces, Him whose light shines upon them and who can be characterised by the fact that aside from Him none of these things would have the order they plainly possess. Contradictory views of the universe are part of the conflict of truth with error. Truth must prevail over falsehood by dint of sound thought or by the strength of the case outweighing its weakness.

But, beyond that, thought on the essence of the creator, or the demand to know the essence—these are interdicted to human reason. For there is, as we know, a complete otherness between the two existences, and the Divine Being is immune from all compositeness. To ask to know it is totally to overextend the power man possesses and is a vain and dangerous enterprise. It is in fact a delusion because it essays the inconceivable and a danger because it conduces to an offence against faith, involving a will to definition of the indefinable and the limitation of the illimitable.

The tradition already quoted and thus far invoked applies with no less force to the attributes as to the Divine essence. They are alike both included in the veto on, and the impossibility of, the attempt to fathom them. All the knowledge we may have of them is that God is so characterized. But their ultimate significance it is within His exclusive possession to know. Our minds have no competence there. Thus the Qur'ān and earlier Scriptures confine themselves to directing attention to the creator's existence and to His perfect attributes, as these may be known from the contemplation of the created world. As for the nature of His attributes and what they signify, it is beyond our province to discuss.

What we are bound to believe, then, is that God is known to exist, inalienably Himself above all creatures, from eternity to eternity, living, knowing, willing, almighty, unique in His necessary existence, unique in the perfection of His attributes and the one and only maker of His creation, that He speaks, that He is all-hearing, all-aware, and characterized by all those other attributes of which the sacred law tells by ascription of names to Him.

But as for whether the attributes are other or more than the essence, whether speech is an attribute other than the import of the heavenly books within the Divine knowledge, and whether hearing and seeing in God are other than His knowledge of things heard and seen, and other such controversial issues, of the pundits and the contentions of the schools—all these are questions impenetrable to us, beyond the wit of human mind to attain. Even the effort to shed light on them at all by citation from the holy text is a mental task entirely beyond our capacity and does despite to the sacred law. For linguistic usage does not 'grasp' truth, and even if words do come to expressive grips with reality, the way language puts things never does full justice to them as they really are essentially. Even the most exemplary of the philosophic schools—when they are not astray—quite fail to bring assurance. We must take our position within the limits of reason and ask God's forgiveness for those who believed in Him and in the revelations of His messengers and yet engaged in these vain debates.

Chapter 5

THE ACTS OF GOD MOST HIGH

As set down above, the acts of God derive from His knowledge and will, and whatever issues from knowledge and will is freely chosen. Nothing that proceeds from choice is obligatory to the free in essence in His choosing. None of His deeds proceed from Him of necessity as He essentially is. All the attributes of His acts, creation, provision, granting and forbidding, chastisement and beneficence, are affirmed of Him by the special option of power. The intelligent mind, in allowing that all God's actions are by His knowledge and will, would emphatically never entertain the idea that any of His deeds were essentially necessary to His nature, as is the case for example in respect of the necessary qualities of things or of the Divine attributes which have to be necessarily posited of Him. As already indicated, that would be plainly contradictory and impossible.

Something, however, must be said here before we pass on, about those ill-considered articles in which some writers fumble and grope, like brothers who have strayed apart en route to a common destination, and encountering each other again in thick darkness clamour among themselves for direction, each suspecting the other of hostility and violence, with the result that heated battles break out among them, and most of them succumb, and all to no avail. Then when morning breaks, they recognise each other and the survivors recover their right mind. Had they known each other at the outset they would have assisted each other in reaching their destination and would all have attained their goal in brotherly concord and by the clear light of truth.

What we have in mind in recalling this contentious theology in its troubled tensions is the notion that God is of necessity bound to consider the general good in His acts and in His fulfilment of threats against the insubordinate among His creatures, and similar issues classifying His actions under causes and effects. One school of opinion even went so far in putting God under necessity that the student might suspect from their claims that they were reckoning Him under obligation and liability, enjoining Him to get on energetically with the fulfilment of rights and duties appropriate to Him. He is so far exalted above such necessities. Others went to the extreme of denying all causation within His acts so that any one taking stock of their views would imagine that they would like Him variable, establishing today what He violated yesterday, and doing tomorrow the contrary to what He has ruled today, or merely negligent and reckless about the entail of His actions. 'Praise be to the Lord, whose power far transcends the notions they imagine.' Wiser than all rule, truer than all speaking, God's majesty and the purity of His religion are higher and worthier than all these imputings.

All are agreed that the acts of God are always in wisdom. Even the extremists, as well as those who take a mediating position, alike hold the view that there is nothing frivolous about the acts of God or deceptive in His world. Yet despite this agreement they started feuding and disputing over the text and its meanings, without reaching any clear terminus. It is up to us to take what they are agreed about and bring this discordant strife back to the truth in its oneness.

The wisdom of a deed lies in its conducing directly to the preservation of order or restraining both particular and general corruption. It also means that, as perceptible to rational mind from any intelligible aspect, the deed is neither bootless nor frivolous. Any other alleged definition of wisdom must be referred back to the issue of what words mean and the self evident quality of reason. What engenders action cannot be called wisdom or be rationally so classified, if the action does not issue from the conscious intention of the doer. For then the sleeper could be counted wise who killed a scorpion, about to sting a child, with a chance movement in his sleep, or with such a motion drew back a child from a pit in which he was on the point of falling. Indeed, by this sort of criterion many dumb animals could be accounted wise, if some particular or general

The Acts of God 59

benefit resulted from their random movements. But it would be nonsense to say so.

There is one sound principle admitted by all rational men, namely that 'the deeds of an intelligent agent are never pointless or idle'. In this dictum what they mean by an intelligent agent is one who knows in his willing the intended consequence of his action. They mean by its being safe-guarded from pointlessness simply the fact that it will only undertake acts the results of which lie within its intention. If this is so in respect of merely human agents, how much more, do you suppose, with the author of mind and the uttermost of perfection in knowledge and will? All this is conceded by everyone and does not admit of controversy.

'The handiwork of God Who has rightly disposed all things . . .' (Surah 27.88), and 'made His creation excellent', is full of examples of His wise competence. There is the order of the heavens and the earth and all that they contain, the pattern of the whole universe in its preservation, its immunity from the disorder which would bring it into nothing-ness, the fidelity which assures the well-being of all that exists, whether of living things like plants and animals, and each specifically within its nature. Were there not these marvels of wisdom, evidence of God's knowledge would in no way be hard to come by.

This Divine wisdom which we now know by virtue of everything having its place and of the satisfaction of the needs that are, must be understood as either consciously and by volition at work in its doings, or not. But the negative position is impossible. For it would involve an assertion of limited knowledge, if the action was not known, or else some negligence if it was not willed. We have early affirmed that His knowledge embraces everything and that it is impossible for any effect to be outside His will. He intends the action and intends what the ordering wisdom effectuates. This only makes sense if He really wills what He orders, since His wisdom in ordering belongs to the deed. It is inconceivable that His wise ordering should not will the deed consciously in view of its connection with it. We must hold the conviction that His acts cannot be without wisdom unto execution and that this wisdom cannot possibly be other than willed. As we have said earlier, if we were to credit the wild notion that what action achieves is unwilled, we should not be talking about wisdom.

The necessity of wisdom in His works belongs with the necessity of perfection in His knowledge and will—a truth which has never been in dispute. The same is to be said of the necessity of His promises and retributions being realized. For they belong with the perfection of His knowledge, will and truth. For He is the most truthful of utterers. The contents of the Qur'ān and the Sunnah which may be taken to the contrary must be referred back to the rest of the verses and to other traditions, so that the whole may be applied in accord with clear axioms already noted, and in harmony with the perfection of God, His surpassing wisdom and greatness. The fundamental principle to which all the purport of this chapter leads is in the saying: 'We have not created the heavens and the earth and all betwixt them in jest. Had We willed to find amusement We would have found it of Ourselves. We cast truth at falsehood until truth triumphs and falsehood is no more. Woe shall befall you for what you impute to God falsely' (Surah 21.16–18).

The words 'We would have found it of Ourselves' mean that from the essence of utter and absolute perfection, to which no lack can be ascribed, would be derived the 'foolish universe'. This is impossible. The word 'if' in this verse: 'If We had being doing such a thing' is an excluding negative: it is identical, that is, with the drift of all that we have here argued.

Those—to continue—who tackle these issues are divided into two groups. There are some who are eager for knowledge of them out of intellectual desire and pleasure. This group gives meanings their names without considering whether or not they are legitimately applicable in respect of God. They call, for example, Divine ordaining wisdom, purpose, end, final cause, providential concern. They find some inward reluctance to curb their pens and refrain from using a word when it seems to them valid. They say that something is God's duty, instead of that it is necessary to Him (difference of preposition) without heeding what may be implied by these terms.

The other group, with less temerity, are aware they are dealing with a religion and religious adherence, with a creed

The Acts of God

relating to God most great, whom men worship with praise and adoration. One must be vigilant for His transcendent honour and abstain, if need be, from language for fear of some impairing word, and steer clear of all such expressions, whether single or multiple. To speak of duty resting upon God suggests obligation and constraint. Or in another phrase it may suggest duress and susceptibility to pressure. To speak of the charge of the general well-being is to introduce the notion of active investigation and pondering—which both, in their turn, imply some deficiency in knowledge. Words like purpose, final cause, aim, suggest an impulse within the soul of the doer from before the genesis to the conclusion of the deed, with the same implication as before. Rather God is most great. But is it right that ventures of thought or restrained diffidence of language should be a cause of division and rancour among believers and lead in the end to the sort of cleavages which now obtain?

Chapter 6

THE DEEDS OF MAN

The man of sound mind and sense knows and affirms of himself that he exists and needs no guide or teacher to bring him to this conclusion. It is the same precisely with his awareness of his actions of will. He weighs them and their consequences in his mind and evaluates them in his will, and then effectuates them by an inward power. To deny any of this would be tantamount to a denial of his existence itself, so opposed would it be to rational evidence.

No less surely does he admit the same features exactly in those who like himself are possessed of sound mind and sound sense. However, it may be that he will anger a friend in the very will to please him or lose what he sets out to acquire. He may endeavour to save himself and fall prey to destruction. If, in such cases, he has not properly directed his mind to the weighing of his act, he will blame himself and take his initial disappointment as a subsequent guide. He will come back to the action in a surer way and with wiser means. Should his failure in the enterprise be due to the competition of a rival for the same end, he will kindle with indignation against him, for his intervention, recognizing in the other the source of his frustration. Conflict will break out. Sometimes he will direct his analysis to a more lofty point. If it is not the intrusion of a rival or his own incapacities which account for the failure he suffers, but rather, for example, a storm of wind wrecking his merchandise, or a thunderbolt destroying his cattle or the death of some helper on whom his hopes rested, or the removal from office of a person of importance—such factors will direct his thoughts to a force in the world beyond the control of his own powers. He will come to realise that there is an authority outside his own reach and beyond his disposition. When the facts in all their unmistakable reality have brought home to him that events in the world are in their entirety derived from a necessarily existent Being ordering them according to His knowledge and will, man will submit with reverence and humility, and come to terms with his situation in that light. But with that he will keep in mind his own share in events. The believer witnesses to the evident and visible proof of the power of the creator of all and knows it higher than the power of contingent beings. He confesses in like manner that in all his acts of choice, whether rational or physical, he is proceeding upon powers and capacities given to him by God for these ends. Man's proper gratitude for God's benefits is inculcated in the words: 'Thankfulness is the servant's use of all that God has bestowed upon him in such wise as to fulfil its creative ends'.

This is the foundation of the law's provisions. By this the Divine ordinances are effectuated. To deny these things is to deny the faith itself and the place therein of mind, which God has honoured by addressing it in His commands and prohibitions.

However, to discuss further the reconciliation between the Divine prescience and the Divine will, already proved, and the evident power of human choice, is to attempt to penetrate the secret of *Qadar*, or destiny. In this we are forbidden to involve ourselves. It is useless to busy our minds with what they can scarcely attain. Those in every religious community, and especially among Christians and Muslims, who over-step the bounds in this field, find that when all argument is done they are back where they started. All they have achieved is division and disunity. Among them are the champions of the complete freedom of man, the servant, over all his actions and his absolute independence. This is a manifest delusion. Others have asserted *Jabr*, or pre-determination, with or without naming it so. But this is a destructive notion inimical to the sacred law and tending to the extinction of the ordinances of morality. It is a final proscription of rational judgement which is the pillar of faith.

There are those who claim that belief in man's 'acquisition' *kasb* of his actions leads to the sin of *Shirk* against God, which is, of course, the supreme wrong. But such views have not taken account of the Quranic significance of *Shirk* and its meaning in the Sunnah. It is the belief that any other than God has a superior causation to that which God, by His gift, has set in the manifest causes and that there can be a greater force than that arising from the created order. It is the belief of those who exalt other than God to Divine authority and who presume to dispense with the means that He has given, such as military forces as the condition of victories in war, or the use of medicines given by God for the purpose of healing sicknesses, or the paths and precepts He has ordained whereby happiness might be ours in this world and the next. To seek these and similar ends in wilful neglect of the Divine means is a form of the sin of *Shirk*, or not letting God be God.

It was this which characterized the heathen and all their ilk. To end it once and for all was the mission of Islam in returning back to God alone the authority in all realms—an authority beyond and above all human competence and created causes. Islam laid down two great points as twin pillars of happiness and human activity. The first is that man the servant acquires the means to happiness by his will and capacity. The second is that the Divine authority lies behind this acquisition as that from which all existents derive. It is this authority in its effects which intervenes between man and the realization of his wishes. There is nothing, aside from God, with the power to bring man help in respect of what is not feasible within his *kasb*.

The sacred law came to affirm these things and to forbid man to seek for aid except in his creator, gladly accomplishing his actions after alert assessment of them. It summoned him to set his sights on God alone for succour while exerting himself to the full in ensuring right thinking and sound doing. Both faith and reason agree that man cannot rightly do otherwise.

It was these things which guided the early pioneers of the Islamic community, in exploits which astounded the peoples at large. Among later speculative thinkers, Abū-Ma'ālī al-Juwaynī, Imām al-Ḥaramain, based himself also upon them, although some who failed to understand him have denied it.

Let me say again, faith in the Divine unity requires of the believer only that his powers are from God's hand, that he 'acquires' his faith and the other religious works which God has enjoined, that the power of God transcends all human com-

The Deeds of Man

petence and has alone the supreme authority over all the desires of men and their realization, whether by voiding the obstacles or ordering the operative factors which elude either the knowledge or the will of man.

To pursue the matter further and pry into its mysterious elements is, as we have shown, no part of the province of faith. It is also an evil from the rational point of view to seek the lifting of the curtain of these secrets. I do not deny that some assiduous and persistent souls have thereby attained points of view which satisfy them and slake their perplexities. But they are few indeed. And, moreover, such light God gives truly to whom He wills, to the disciples of devotion and purity. There are the many who deceive themselves, and there are those whose notions have very mischievous effects in the present-day condition of the community.

Were it my wish I could go much further and say that the very diversities evident in the created world are the supreme work of a wise providence. Differentiation only happens when particularities require it. It is the same with types. The giver of existence has endowed the various kinds and types in accordance with what they are. Each being has its peculiar characteristics. Man is one of these. Among his distinguishing features by which he is different from other animals are his capacity for thought and his ability to choose his actions in line with his thinking. It is with his being, as given to him, that these distinctive qualities belong. If he were to be deprived of any of them he would become, perhaps, an angel, or some animal. When we say that he is man with that gift of being which is humanity, this in no way means that there is any compulsoriness about his actions. The Divine knowledge is the context of what the human will effectuates. It is aware he will do such and such action at such and such a time—a good deed to be rewarded, for example, and that he will do this or that evil and be appropriately requited. His works are throughout the consequence of his 'acquisition' and choice. Nothing in (Divine) knowledge dispossesses man of his option-taking in 'acquisition'. The fact that what is in the Divine knowledge must inevitably befall arises from its being actual, and that which is so is not susceptible of being changed.

A most apposite analogy is available in our empirical knowledge. A person who takes part in a rebellion knows assuredly that his revolt against the sovereign, which he makes of his own volition, will inevitably incur retribution. He nevertheless engages in it and becomes liable to such requital. Nothing in his knowledge, which certainly accords with the facts, has the least effect on his chosen line of conduct, either by way of deterrence or compulsion. A clear awareness of the facts on the part of the knower is not, at the bar of reason, a proper constraint or hindrance. This is a matter in which the flux and diversity of terms causes misconceptions.

It would readily be possible to amplify this demonstration in the hope that it would commend itself to any perceptive mind which had not let its acumen be corrupted by terminological wrangles. But I am dissuaded from doing so by the simple fact that a sound faith has no need of it. The minds of common people will anyway be inadequate for the essentials of the matter in question, irrespective of the length to which the exponent may take it in clarification. The larger part of the specialists are afflicted with the disease of traditionalism (*taqlīd*). They believe and then demand proof, but only on condition that the proof shall agree with their belief. If they are confronted with what counters their belief they will have nothing to do with it. Indeed, they oppose it tooth and nail, even if it means jettisoning rationality altogether. The way of most of them is first to dogmatise and then to lay claim to proof. Rarely one finds among them any who first prove and then believe. If anybody cries loud enough in the depths of these surmisings: 'Woe to the stumbler!' that is enough to overturn the whole Sunnah of God and His creation, and to falsify His guidance in the sacred law. After a bout of apprehension, they recover their composure in the shelter of the familiar. 'We take our stand only on the familiar, and only in God is there power and strength, the most high, the mighty.'

GOOD AND EVIL DEEDS

The voluntary actions of men belong to the category of actual existents and are within our comprehension. Our susceptibility to them, when our senses record them or we reproduce the mental image of them, is exactly akin to our experience when we react to any material occurrences within our sense experience or our imagination. This is evident enough and can dispense with proof.

We find essentially, within ourselves the faculty of distinction between what is beautiful and what is ugly. Schools of opinion differ among men over the beauty of women, and women too differ about the beauty of men. But no one differs about the fact of beauty, say in the colour of flowers or in the array of foliage in plants and trees, especially if the arrangement of the flowers harmonizes and assorts the colours in the truest relation. Nor is anyone likely to dispute the ugliness present in a clash of ill-ordered and jumbled things. Our sense of beauty gives vent to itself in delight and wonder, and ugliness is greeted with disgust and dismay. This discrimination between beauty and ugliness applies alike to things seen, heard, touched, tasted and smelled. The sense perceptions we all have make these things familiar to everyone.

This is not the place to attempt a definition of beauty and its antithesis. But it will be universally agreed that man, and indeed certain animals, have the faculty of distinguishing the two. On this ability rest the works of art in their variety and culture, in its manifold forms, has progressed to its present level thereby. Tastes may differ—but things *are* either beautiful or ugly.

As has been said, this is unmistakably so of the objects of sense perception. Perhaps it is not so plainly evident in the insensible world of the mind where the recognition of beauty is more elusive and indefinable. In the immaterial world of the necessary Being and of the 'subtle' spirits and also of the qualities of the human soul, perfection belongs with a beauty accessible only to those who have a mind for it and whose awakened contemplation it quite ravishes. Imperfection has an ugliness undeniable to the high-minded, even though the emotional reactions in certain cases differ from those pertaining to ugliness in the sensible world. Will any deny the 'ugliness' of intellectual deficiency, of a weakness of nerve? The victims of these imperfections strive to conceal them and even boast at times that they have the opposite character—which in itself seems enough to prove our contention.

What is ugly, however, may derive some beauty from its effects, and likewise the beautiful may acquire ugliness by association. Myrrh is a repellent and bitter-tasting thing. Some deformed, misshapen king no one will admire. Nevertheless the good effect of myrrh in treating disease, or the justice of the hunchback among his subjects or his magnanimous relations towards you—these may change your attitude. Thus beauty of effect may set that from which it flows in more agreeable light and even its physical manifestation will be taken for admirable. So much could be said, in reverse, for the foulness of what is sweet if it has harmful effects. The soul finds beauty repugnant when it tyrannizes and injures.

Is it possible for a sound intelligence not to speak of voluntary deeds of men in the same terms as of material things? Though differentiated from the latter, they come within our sense experience and our mental conceptions, either in themselves or through their consequences. Our souls are susceptible to what they are and mean, just as we are to the images of the external world. It is surely clear that they are part of existent things and are to be assessed by the same criteria.

Deeds of human choice can evoke the same sort of admiration as physically beautiful things, such as the rhythmic movements of an army on parade or the motions of skilful players in games, or as we now say gymnastics, or the rhythm of music sung by a master. There are other actions which have an inherently ugly quality, stirring the same kind of sensation as the sight of some disorder in creation, like the confusion of the weak-minded in face of anxiety or the lamentations of the female mourners and the cries of the despairing.

There are also those actions which are repugnant because of the suffering to which they give rise. Others are good in that they bring about pleasure and forestall pain. Among the first are blows and wounds and all human actions that inflict pain. Among the second are eating in hunger and drinking in thirst and all the innumerable things which enable pleasure and obviate suffering. From this angle the beautiful would be equated with what makes for pleasure, and the ugly what makes for pain.

The Deeds of Man

Human discrimination between good and bad, in these two senses, differs little from the distinction made by the higher animals, except in emotional intensity and in the greater range and 'definition' of man's assessment of the beautiful and the ugly.

Some voluntary actions are evaluated with reference to the benefit that accrues from them or from the harm they entail. This form of discrimination in its highest manifestation is unique to man. Only seldom do animals share this capacity with man and only in its inferior aspects. For it is a peculiarity of mind and a secret of the Divine wisdom in the gift of thought.

There are, of course, pleasurable things which are found bad in their consequences, like excess in food and drink, perpetual listening to music and free rein in the indulgence of passions. These are deleterious to health. They waste the intellect and dissipate wealth, bringing on feebleness and ignominy. In this context the evil of the pleasant lies in the length of the one compared with the brevity of the other—so long in fact that there may be no returning back from suffering, ending even in death itself, perhaps in the direst form. For there is a terrible discrepancy between the scant enjoyment and the grievous pain.

There are occasions of suffering which are to be seen as good things. We put up with toilsomeness in our labours for the sake of the livelihood we acquire and the ensuring of our needs in times of weakness. To strive against lusts and to endure hardness from time to time in abstaining from pleasure conserves our powers of body and mind for their proper enjoyment of proportioned pleasures in a fashion that will be free from vacillation and trouble. In this way too we lighten the distresses of life—vale of tears as it may well be deemed.

Also among the pain-making things which human intelligence has considered good are a man's joining battle against his enemy, whether from his own kin or beyond it, in self-defence or in defence of those with identity of interests, such as his father's sons, or his tribe, or his people or community, according to the degree of his sense of obligation. In this he risks even life itself, as if he saw in the laying down of life a sure means to another's life. In spirit he is well aware of this even though his reason cannot give it shape. We may also include in this category the toils and labours men undergo to discover what the still unknown facts of the universe hold for science, esteeming the exactingness involved as nothing in comparison with the pleasure and peace of mind which come with truth in so far as they are able for it.

One pleasure worthy of being judged despicable is to lay hands on what another man's efforts have gained him and to allay one's hatreds by destroying or despoiling the object we dislike. Such deeds give rise to a general disquiet which may come to affect even the perpetrator himself. The reader may visualize for himself what is involved in loyalty to agreements and bonds and by their repudiation.

All this has been familiar enough to human reason which has classified the harmful and the beneficial, calling the former evil-doing and the latter well-doing. This distinction is the source of that between virtue and vice, defined diversely by the scholars, both in sum and in detail, the definitions varying with the quality of the scholar's intelligence. The two have been made to hinge upon human happiness and misery in this life, or they have equally been tied to the civilized human order and its disruption, the greatness of the nations and their depravity, or their strength and weakness. However, only by a few thinkers have really adequate definitions been reached.

All these observations are rudimentary matters of reason about which no philosopher or schoolman quarrels. Voluntary actions are good or bad in themselves or by reference to their particular or general consequence. Sense and reason are well able to distinguish the two in the above respects, without having to rely upon instruction. One pointer to that lies in the observed facts of some species of animal and the evidence we have of the behaviour of small children prior to any rational cognizance of the meaning of law. It is one of the lessons of man's history and of what we know about him in his days of ignorance.

It is good to recall at this point what a certain scientist observed about ants. A group of ants were constructing a house and one of the ants, who seemed to be superintending, noticed that the workers had set the roof too low. She gave the order to pull the whole down. This was done and the edifice then reconstructed to the proper height, with the new and higher roof made from the rubble of the old. Such is the power of distinction between the harmful and the beneficial. He who claims that actions are not good and bad in an absolute way has filched away his own intelligence and reduced himself to a stupidity below the ants.

We have already said that the necessary Being and His perfect attributes are rationally known. However, if a 'rationalist' succeeded in proving the necessary Being and His attributes as they are, apart from revelation and did so unaided by any prophetic mission, as some among men have done, and, from study of his own make-up as a self, proceeded to the belief that the rational principle in man survives death as some other peoples have come to believe, and if, going on further, rightly or wrongly, he sought to claim that this survival of the human soul after death meant either bliss or wretchedness, and, further again, he based these on the knowledge of God and virtuous living, or an ignorance of God and viciousness of life, respectively, and so constructed a scheme of works serviceable or inimical to the soul after death, what rational or dogmatic principle would there then be to deny the 'rationalist' the claim that since the knowledge of God is imperative and all virtues, with their consequent deeds, are obligatory, and since vices with their entail are forbidden, he is justified in laying down any rules he likes and calling the rest of humanity to accept his belief and adopt the same pattern of behaviour as himself? Without any revealed law to deter him, it would be difficult to disqualify such a chain of assumption.

These presuppositions, however, are not borne out by what we know of mankind in general. On the contrary, it is not believed universally that the knowledge of God is needful or that the crux of eternal happiness lies in virtue and of eternal misery in evil doing. Such universality of belief sound intelligence can affirm.

Were human needs and fears limited as in the case, say, of elephants and lions, and were human intelligence confined to such wants, man had doubtless found it possible to identify the profitable and evade the harmful, in a way requiring no individual variation, with happiness resulting and every one secure from evil arising from his fellow, and even the animal kingdom immune from depredations.

But man's very humanity means that by a necessary law of his nature his needs refuse to be held within such bounds. His being is not peculiar to any single climate or location. He is, rather, endowed with thinking powers that are more than adequate for his employment in the satisfaction of needs unlimited to any special station or context. These faculties, enriching his pleasures, manifest themselves in a wide variety of forms and effects. They are as endlessly diverse as is humanity itself, with its medley of races, types and people. Were it otherwise man would only differ from the animals in having an erect stature and remarkable hands.

God has given to man in possession three faculties in which he is distinguished from the animals—memory, imagination and reflective thought. Memory preserves from the past pictures that are obscured by the preoccupations of the present. It brings to mind the images of things desirable or reprehensible, as these are aroused by actual resemblances or contrasts. Clearly, one may remember because the immediate scene brings a parallel or a sharp contrast to one's notice. Imagination gives shape to these recollections and to their attendant circumstances, with a sort of present immediacy, and evokes a pattern of future pleasure or pain from the precedents of the past, and urges the spirit either to seek or to evade it, the means to which are found by turning to the third endowment of man, namely reflective thought.

On these three faculties rests the happiness of man. They are likewise the fount and source of his misery.

Some people have a balanced memory, a steady imagination and a sound intelligence. Take a man taking critical stock of a pattern of prodigal living in which he has uselessly squandered his resources. He recalls the suffering of some earlier time of privation and visualizes anew the value of money and the enjoyment it enables, whether by way of meeting wants or repulsing the pains he feels at the sight of poverty in others, and providing the wherewithal to meet the situation. He bethinks himself of how he may come by money once again, but without trespassing on other men's rights. He turns his thoughts to its acquisition by honest effort in the use of the powers that are God's gift and by dint of the natural energies he can harness to his ends.

Another man, however, sees this world's goods in the hands of another, abandons the path of rectitude, calls to mind the kind of pleasure he formerly enjoyed from just such material resources and visualises a much ampler future enjoyment of them. Such kindling and exaggerating imagination casts its shadow over his thoughts and obscures the sound forms of acquisition. He starts to rely on force and guile, stealing from the wealthy in order to spend freely on what he imagines to be his advantage. He thus ruins his own powers and flouts the order of human security entrusted by God to His servants. Such a man has invoked the law of Cain. It will be no easy thing either for himself or others to bring back the trustful securities which his criminal conduct has breached.

A glance at human behaviour is enough to show into which of these two patterns men fall. The force or frailty of memory, the passion or moderation of the imagination, the crookedness or integrity of the mind—these are the supreme factors in the distinction between what promotes well-being and what engenders evil consequences, whether in persons or in their deeds. Imagination, thought, and memory, too, are in turn greatly affected by temperament, atmosphere and personal environment of family and friends.

People are at one in saying that actions are either beneficial or harmful. The essential goodness or badness of things intelligence, sound study and a balanced disposition can always identify. By them we attain to the truth of the moral order. It is also agreed that good actions are those from which abiding benefit accrues even if the initial effect is painful, while evil actions are those which conduce to the disruption of the personality or its relationships and environment, even if there is in them a great sense of present well-being. People differ, though, in assessing individual instances, according to their temperament, their nature, their upbringing and their whole setting. So it is that men tend towards evil of every kind in the supposition that they are seeking the useful and eluding the harmful. The mind alone is not of itself adequate to bring man to the source and ground of happiness in this life, except in rare cases which time has not recorded. If their great significance has in measure made them known, they have been very few and far between. We have already said something of them.

Human minds are not uniformly able to know God or the life to come. Though they share a common sense of submission to a power higher than their own and most men feel there is another age beyond this one, heathenism has disordered their thoughts and deflected them from the path of blessedness. Generally speaking, the human mind is not competent to know, of God, what ought to be known, nor to understand properly the nature of the life to come, nor yet to comprehend the requital which every sort of action will receive in that world. Only a few have so attained, and they are those to whom God has given a perfect reason and the light of perception, despite their not having the boon of prophetic guidance and example. These would have been the first to have joined his ranks had any prophet reached them. Perhaps by their own thinking they have come to the point of Divine knowledge, albeit from an angle it is not in fact well to take in the contemplation of the majesty on high.

Other aspects of the life to come which the human mind cannot embrace of itself alone have to do with the significance of the pleasures and pains there and the ways of reckoning that apply there. In no particular are these within our knowledge.

There are many actions which it is impossible to interpret precisely so as to show how and why they are beneficial or otherwise in their sequel. This is true whether we think of those effects within or beyond this life. Take, for example, the several matters of ritual prescription, the number of the ritual acts of prayer (*raka'āt*) or the Islamic pilgrimage ceremonies and the various celebrations belonging to the Mosaic religion, as well as invocatory intercession and practices of asceticism in the Christian religion (*'Īsāwiyyah*)—the human mind cannot know or explain the clue to the efficacy of these forms of worship. God only knows their relation to the welfare of man.

In all these respects, and in the exercise of its powers of thought and physique towards the goal of its utmost good in both worlds, the human spirit needs a helper, to whom it can have recourse. It must reach out to such a guide if it is rightly to interpret human conduct, truly to affirm the Divine attributes and adequately to know the shape of the world to come. In a word it must learn the way to blessedness in both time and eternity from some source beyond itself. Yet such a helper could have no 'writ' of his own except as he took part in human nature. Only so would his message be intelligible. He would also need to be distinguished from the rest of mankind by a quality quite other than the commonplace and the natural order of things. Such extraordinary status would assure his hearers that he spoke from God and truly had access to the knowledge of man's needs. He would also need to be adequately mindful of the perfect attributes of God and know of the life of the world to come and its expectations. What otherwise the minds of men would be quite unable to apprehend through frailty of conception they will be helped to learn, with the resolution of their perplexities, through reliance upon the interpretations of a spokesman from God, the all-knowing, the ever-aware.

Chapter 7

THE PROPHET AS THE HELPER

Prophecy defines the attributes of the necessary Being and does so adequately in satisfying man's need of knowledge. To those of superior capacity it shows the degree of awareness to which they can attain in surpassing their lesser fellows. But only what is genuinely accessible to the generality of men is required as essential. We have earlier expounded the existence of God and His unity and His attributes and it was these the prophecies came to invite men to confess. They directed humanity to ways whereby these truths could be plainly demonstrated. Only by dint of the revealed law do we have knowledge of obligation and of the good in that quality of certainty which brings peace to the soul. Likewise we only know from the same source how to identify and repudiate the ignorance and unbelief which reject what the sacred law enjoins or disapproves. If the human mind were to dispense with the law it would lack the requisite assurance, the strong conviction and the certitude, on which secure belief is built. Only by the Divine law do we know the obligatory quality of the precepts to which the promises of reward and the reality of retribution relate. There is, of course, in these no suggestion that the knowledge of God is not good in and for itself. The law simply comes to disclose things as they are and not, so to speak to *make* them so. Its own texts bear this out.

I will cite one example from many. God said by the mouth of Joseph: 'Are numerous lords better than God, the One, the supreme?' (Surah 12.39). Clearly what he is saying here is that diversity of gods divides men in their search for the greatest they can find to invoke beyond their own powers. Each party becomes fanatically competitive about what it has espoused. This partisanship corrupts all their behaviour, as is only too plain. On the other hand a common faith in a single God brings

The Prophet as the Helper

these factions into a single unity under one authority and one undisputed rule. Therein community is shaped in brotherhood and with it the ground of men's well-being. As I believe, men will come back to this if only at long last. In this way, the sacred law came requiring belief: it also came as a guide to the good that is through the faith.

Prophecy defines the works on which men's happiness depends in both time and eternity: in God's name it appeals to men to hold to the bounds which God has set. Oftentimes it shows them aspects of the beautiful and the vile in the commands and prohibitions of God. The obligation to perform its injunctions and counsels and to shun what it forbids or deplores, in line with the prescriptions of the sacred law and in the light of that law's assurance of the due rewards and punishments, constitutes a sum of knowledge which is not feasible to unaided reason. It is the sacred law which brings it. That fact, however, is not to say that the burden of the law's commands is not in itself good. It is, indeed, good, for it leads to our well-being in this world and the next and has a benign bearing on our affairs, on our bodily health and on our security of spirit, of property, and of reputation, and in uniting our hearts more closely to God. All this is particularized in the contents of the law. There may well be also actions whose good quality cannot be recognised, and forbidden things where the evil in view is not definable by us. In those cases the goodness and badness consist simply in the fact of the command and the evil lies in the fact of the prohibition. For God knows all.

PROPHETIC MISSION IN GENERAL

By *Al-Risālah*, or prophetic message, is meant in general the sending of apostles to bring to us doctrines and ordinances from God, the creator of men, who gives to them, as to other creatures, what they need for the fulfilment and satisfaction of their being in all its aspects.

The elaboration of this theme falls into two parts. The first and the simpler to discuss is that such belief in the mission of the messengers is a pillar of the faith. Every believer, man and woman, must hold the faith that God has sent messengers, from among men, proclaiming both God's reward of the good and His retribution of the evil. They fulfilled their communication to their peoples as was laid upon them by bringing home God's essential transcendence, His almighty power over men His servants, and His detailed commandments as to the good works and qualities He demands, as well as the evil actions and ways He has forbidden. Every believer must hold the faith that the messengers ought to be believed, as bringing this their message truly from God, and that it is incumbent to model ourselves on their pattern of conduct, fulfilling what they have commanded and eschewing what they prohibit. It is also to be believed that some of the messengers received books sent down to them, containing what God wanted them to communicate, informing men of Him and of the limits and injunctions by conformity to which He would teach men their good. It is a matter of faith that these sacred revealed books in their hands are truth, and that the messengers were aided by a Divine protection not accorded to rational minds and human abilities. This quality of revealed books, transcending as it does the knowledge of ordinary mankind, is what is meant by matchlessness or miracle, the inimitability which is the proof of the prophetic veracity. When the messenger claims prophethood and demonstrates it by this *Mu'jizah* or surpassingness, it becomes obligatory to accept his message and mission.

Necessarily, inseparable from this is the duty of belief in their exceptional nature (*fitrah*) or endowment, the soundness of their reason and the trustworthiness of their words, their fidelity in the communication of their message and their immunity from all that degrades human behaviour, as well as their freedom in the body from all that is unseemly and gross. It is to be believed also that they are above everything that is inimical to these qualities. They partake in such measure in the soul of the Divine splendour that no human kind can presume against them any spiritual charge. They are, withal, purely human and subject to the same experiences as the rest of men. They eat and drink and sleep: they may be inattentive or forgetful in what is unrelated to their mission. They fall ill and become the victims of wrongdoing and of persecution, even to the point, with some prophets, of death itself.

The Prophet as the Helper

The revelatory wonder is not rationally to be classified as an impossibility. For the contravening of the familiar, natural pattern of things is not something susceptible of proof as to its impossibility. We might liken it in this connection to what happens when a sick man is prevented from eating for a time. Were a healthy man to abstain so long from food he would die, whereas despite the aggravation of weakness and the wastage by fasting, the sick man survives.

It will be said that this is doubtless owed to the fact of another natural law. Our claim is that He who shaped the law is He who gave the creatures being. It is in no way impossible for Him to lay down special laws for what contravenes normal processes. We cannot penetrate to the end in view but we can at least discern its effects in those whom God has specially favoured. Once we have believed that He is the maker of the universe, almighty and free, it is simple for us to know that nothing can prevent Him from conforming what happens in time to any pattern, and for any cause He pleases within His foreknowledge.

The miracle of matchlessness in the Qur'ān is inevitably involved in challenge and controversy where there are claims to prophethood. For the pretender will assert that it is there, discernible and confirmatory, in his deliverances. The prophet will rely on it to sustain his claim to be *bona fide* a messenger from God—a claim which will be vindicated by God's affording the *mu'jizah* to him at that time. For it is impossible that God should confirm a liar. For to support a liar would be to make him credible and to assert truth in a liar is itself lying and this is impossible to God. When, therefore, the miracle is evident, super-human as it is, its presence constitutes a corroboration of the claims. We may know absolutely that God has only made it evident as an attestation of him with whom it appears, however much this may be denied by the arrogant.

As for magic and the like, though we may concede that its manifestations transcend physical causation, it remains, for all that, in the realm of contingency and is in no sense comparable to the miracle of the revealed books.

The prophetic qualities earlier enumerated are necessary to the prophets, inasmuch as if their endowment were of lower worth than that of their contemporaries, or their spiritual vitality were feebler than other men possessed, of if their mentality were in any way deficient, they would not be worthy of the Divine calling to the supreme vocation, namely that to revelatory action and the apprehension of the secrets of Divine knowledge. Were their bodies not free of unseemliness, the resultant disquiet would be an argument for the sceptic to reject their claims. Were they to be liars or traitors or men of ill behaviour, confidence would be weakened, they would be deceivers not directors and their mission would lose all point. It would be the same were they to be negligent or forgetful in respect of their charge to communicate dogmas and rules of life.

As for their liability to error in provinces other than their Divine role and the sacred law, opinions have differed. Some allow the possibility but the major weight of opinion disallows it. Of Muḥammad, for example, tradition says that he at first forbade the pollination of date palms, but subsequently allowed it, in view of the effects of his ban upon the crop. He did so in order to teach men that their practices in such economic and practical fields are the result of their experiments and researches, and that these last are quite valid, so long as the Divine laws are observed and the fine virtues maintained. As for the story about Adam and his disobedience over eating of the tree, the inner reason for the prohibition and for his censure, is not revealed. All that we know on that score is that it was the reason for the peopling of the earth by Adam's race. It is as if the ban and the partaking were double symbols of two aspects of Adam's life and of man's condition. It is God who knows. It is in any event very difficult to come by any rational proof or decisive dogmatic evidence for the view many take about prophetic freedom from error.

Chapter 8

MAN'S NEED OF PROPHETIC MISSION

The previous section has presented the relevant points about the first issue named, that is, what the believer must hold about the messengers. God willing, our discussion here has to do with proving our need of them. This is disputatious territory and treacherous ground, where many thoughts and ideas jostle together. It is not our purpose to discuss the primitive doctrine, nor to expound subsequent thinking. As elsewhere in this book, we confine ourselves to a simple statement of what is believed, by the shortest expository route, without looking into controversially inspired aspects, nor yet into corroboratory positions, except incidentally or by allusion when indispensable.

The proof of human need for the messengers of God moves along two lines. The first, already noted, takes its departure from belief in the survival of the human soul after death and in the fact of another life after this one here below, with blessings to enjoy and painful punishments to suffer. These alternatives depend eternally on deeds done in this fleeting life on earth, whether those deeds are matters of the heart, such as beliefs, purposes and choices, or of the body like forms of worship and the behaviour of man to man.

Humanity is of one mind, whether monotheists or heathen, sectarians or philosophers—all save a negligible minority—that the human soul is immortal and lives on after separation from the body, not dying in the death of mortal transcience. The final death is a kind of womb of hiddenness. Controversy haunts the effort to visualize this survival and the state of the soul therein. There are different schools of thought about how to attempt elucidation. There is the view that talks of transmigration through human bodies or the bodies of animals successively. Others hold that the transmigration ends when the soul has reached a state of perfection. Others believe that when the soul has departed from the body it returns to a spiritual existence, though preserving from its physical existence only the sequel of bliss or tribulation. Others think that it inheres in ethereal bodies more subtle than these earthly ones. The schools also differ as to the nature of future bliss and torment, the delight of the life beyond and the means which make for happiness or avert eternal punishment. There are many competing ideas among the nations, both ancient and modern, which are too numerous to be passed in review.

This universal sense of a life beyond this world, present as it is in all men, learned and ignorant, barbarian and cultured, nomad and settled, old and contemporary, cannot be considered some mental aberration or some figment of the imagination. On the contrary, it is one of the characteristic intuitions of man as man. Just as men are sure that reason and thought are the twin foundations of their continuing existence as mortals, so are they convinced of this enduring of the soul. Some isolated individuals there are who deny to thought and reason any adequacy for the direction of our doings and dispute the capacity of mind to attain conviction in belief and to achieve the unknown. These even go so far as to say that the world only exists in the imagination and its creations. But these are doubters—even of themselves as doubting. Such cranks make no inroads into the validity of the general intuition of the mass of men that thought and reason are the pillars of life and foundations of being until death. Thus intelligence and intuition alike are sure that this brief life-span is not the sum total of man's existence. Rather man takes off this body of flesh, as he does his clothes, and is alive still in another guise, though its nature be beyond our ken.

That intuitive belief almost vies in clarity with evident proof. Every soul feels that it was created with a readiness for eternal meanings, infinite and unlimited, and with an aspiration for infinite and boundless pleasures, and that it was formed for unbounded growth into perfection. But it also knows with like instinct its exposure to the suffering of conflicting desires and passions, as well as the sallies of bodily disease and all the weight of wind and weather, of needs and a veritable host of adversities of every kind. Amid all these emotions, intuition

Man's Need of Prophetic Mission 83

turns the soul to the belief that the bestower of existence, in all its varied forms, has indeed proportioned the capacities of our being to these needs. He is no frivolous or haphazard conductor of affairs. Since man is entirely primed for unfading knowledge and suffering, for bliss and perfectedness, it cannot be that he endures for limited days and years.

These intuitive feelings stimulate the spirits of men to search into this eternal world and to anticipate how it will be when it is reached, and how too they are to come to it. The answer, both as to what and whither, is obscure and elusive. We are conscious of inadequacy in the deployment of our minds in face of the issues of this brief existence here. They do not suffice to give us the right directions or make good our need for teaching and guidance. We must appeal to the gathered judgement of the ages in assessing our thoughts and correcting our views, in making our emotions truer and our intelligence surer. And today, we are still in unresolved uncertainty about this earthly life, yearning for a quiet assurance still far to seek.

If such be our case in comprehending this life, what is to be hoped from our minds as to the knowledge of the eternal world? Is there at our disposal any guiding experience to bring us to the unseen? Are the ways of thought competent to bring each of us to know what awaits him in the life he is aware he is approaching—and that inexorably? It is a life he has no power whereby to penetrate, and understand its hidden store of fate, and the state in which he will find himself after the dissolution of his mortal life. Nor can he read the hand which holds that destiny in its determination.

Do the methods of speculative thought, with their attendant beliefs and actions, offer any means of certainty? That other world lies all unknown before you. For you that life is shrouded in the deepest mystery. The link between them can hardly be determined by rational study or the reach of intuition. Within us alone is there the mingling of the two worlds. Mere study of our temporal sciences cannot attain to assurance about the realities of the future realms.

Is it not within the wisdom of the creator, He who established man's being on the principles of guidance and doctrine, who made man and taught him the truth and gave him speech for its understanding and writing for mutual expression—is He not able to choose out and appoint from among men in all their diversity a calling of pure honour in those whom He elects from His creation? He surely knows with whom to entrust His message. Is it not in His power to endow them with a uniquely blessed nature and bring their spirits to the perfection appropriate to illumination with the light of Divine knowledge and faithfulness with the trust of His hidden word—that secret which, were it disclosed to others, would mean death to them, or the loss of reason, through its overwhelming majesty? By God's permissive will, the chosen have insight into the unseen world: and they learn what it holds for man. So by their noble office they mediate between the two worlds: they stand on the frontier of the known and the unknown. They live in this world but as not of its people. They are a sort of delegation of the other world, though in fashion unlike its inhabitants. They do God's bidding in telling of His glory. What is hidden from the intellect, about the mysteries of the Divine presence, they proclaim for men to know what God has willed His servants to believe about Him. They tell the Divinely ordained criteria of entrance into eternal blessedness and show men the shape of the world to come as they have need to know it, employing the terms that intelligence can master and keeping within the range of human competence. They bring from God to men the holy laws with their general directives for human conduct, the discipling of men's souls and the restraining of their passions. They teach men what deeds belong with their happiness and their distress in that unknown world—the world that haunts their deepest thoughts in its over-arching reality, but ever eludes their intimate comprehension. The law-telling of the messengers includes all the precepts that belong with the entirety of human action, both outward and inward. God authenticates them with signs beyond the reach of men, in order to reinforce their case and bring final conviction of the truth of the message. So are they truly His messengers, bringing to His creation both good news and admonition.

There can be no doubt that God, who created all things well, making every creature by excellent art, fulfilling every need of every living thing and embracing all from the least to the greatest in His mercy, will hold in His beneficence those to whom He has given this special vocation and for whom He has ordained this access to the knowledge of Himself by the faculty of insight displacing or replacing the normal gifts of ordinary men. He will surely preserve them from dubiety, confusion and error, in what relates to the more significant life of heaven, the more noble of the two states of man.

It is sometimes asked why God has not set within the instinctive capacities of men the knowledge they have need of as their guide to action and to the pathway that leads to the goal in the life beyond. What is this supernatural mercy which brings us direction and instruction as it were by wonders instead of the ordinary capacities? Such interrogatives only come from intellectual pretension and ignorance of the real theme, namely human nature as it really is. They do not penetrate into the fact of how the intellectual spirit truly is and the degree to which persons differ in their abilities. Not every one is ready and able to cope naturally with his every conditions, but needs study and evidence as a basis on which he can deal with his existence. Were man to operate in this instinctive way in respect of his needs, he would be like the animals not like himself. Indeed, he would become a sort of animal, or even like the ant or the bee, or one of the angels who are not of this world of ours.

The second line of evidence for man's need of the prophetic mission is deduced from human nature itself.

History, both ancient and modern, has examples of individual men who have gone apart from their fellows, isolating themselves in woods or on mountains for seclusion. Here they have made friends with the animals, living naturally like the beasts, on grasses and plants, in caves and dens of the earth, letting the rocks and the trees shelter them and taking for clothes the leaves of the trees and the skins of animals that have perished, and thus continuing until the end of their days.

These hermits are like bees who leave the hive and lead their lives away from the normal pattern of their kind. Man, too, is of a species with natural common instincts, pursued within a society of many communities. Each individual, however, has something to do in maintaining the whole, while the community in turn has its role which none can dispense with for his growth and subsistence. There is in each person a feeling that he needs the other members of the community comprehensively as one whole—a fact which needs no lengthy argument, since the history of mankind attests it. A sufficient proof that man always needs to live gregariously is the fact of speech. Only from the need for mutual understanding do we make sense of the tongue with its ready ability to put ideas into words and expressions. There would be no point in mutual comprehension between two or more people if they were free to dispense with one another.

There can, then, be no doubt of this need of the individual for the community. The more the demands of the individual's existence increase, the more his need grows for the contributions of others. This need intensifies and serves to explain the progression from family to tribe and on to nation and mankind as a whole. Our time gives unmistakable evidence of how this involvement through need can extend into the entire human race.

It is just this need for self-preservation, the wish to enjoy the opportunities of life and secure the things that are desirable and repel those that are hateful, which moves the nations—especially those that are truest to their nature—to find relationships and associations that are distinctively their own.

Were men fashioned on the same pattern as the rest of creation, this need we have analysed would surely have been the most benign of factors making for love between persons. For every individual would know thereby that his existence was involved in that of all. He would sense that the collective was a kind of substitute agent for his own powers in harnessing advantages and repelling things inimical. For love is the ground of peace and the messenger of quiet to the heart. It is the motive force by which two in love labour for each other's well-being, stimulating each to defend the other when danger arises. It would have been the prerogative of love to preserve the order of the nations and be the very soul of their perpetuation. It would have been love's to pursue need in line with the order of the universe. For love is the need you feel for the person or the thing you love. In its strongest form we call it passion and ardour.

It is one of the rules of love that it kindles and abides between lovers with the yearning for the inherent and inalienable qualities that belong with its object. But it is only so with human love when it is of the kind that is aroused by the very soul of the beloved and the moral qualities which it cannot forfeit, so that the delight of the encounter is in the love-bond itself and not in any consequent effect. If, however, the exchanges and relations become calculating, the love is changed into a desire to exploit and then relates, not to the source of such advantage, but to the mere advantage itself. Thus there arises between the two parties, instead of love, a possessive power on the one hand and on the other an obsequious fear, or deceit and hypocrisy.

A dog loves his master with a devotion that will defend him to the death. For he is to him the source of all good, in the satisfaction of his needs. The dog associates his satisfying provender and protection with the image of their source. He senses in the loss of the one the loss of the other and so desires his master, literally, for all his life is worth. Even if he passes to another master and is for years away from his first owner and then sees him again in some situation of danger, the sense of the old image will reform and recompose and he will resume a defender's duties with all his strength.

This canine instinct has a single explanation and does not diversify into different ways. The dog's feelings move between his sense of well-being and its origin—they have no other orbit. The need to have his wants met is one with his need for his master who fulfills it. He loves him with a self-love which is not impaired by the service he has to do in return.

As for man—and who really fathoms him?—it is otherwise. He is not a creature who follows intuition without rational cognisance, a mere unthinking centre of emotion. It is the crown of humankind to break out beyond what can be grasped and make unlimited demands. Man refuses to be confined by his littleness but claims release into the bigness of the world in all its majestic immensity. He wrestles with its limitless forces in order to wrest from it the endless benefits it affords. He is possessed of powers of thought and action by which to prevail. He is able thus to set his sights according to his endeavours and ideas. Everything, in consequence, has for him some promise of pleasure: but every pleasure has an attendant pain or fear. So man's desires know no term, and neither do his fears. 'Man was created impatient: when evil befalls him he is despondent but when good fortune comes his way, he grows restive' (Surah 70.19–20).

Humans differ in their capacities of understanding and powers of action; they vary in concentration and resolve. There are those who fall short, being weak or lazy, who nevertheless have avid desires and greedy passions, and see in their fellow man a means to satisfying their wants. Further than that, they picture the pleasure that would be theirs if they had exclusive possession of what is their neighbour's and have with that thought no intention to compensate him with some product of their own labour. For them indeed pleasure lies in enjoying without labouring. In their view the best course is to let clever trickery and cunning devices substitute for hard work, indulging an enjoyment that is totally barren of achievement. They reach the point in this *descensus Averni* where they have no conscience whatever about taking the very life itself from him they are bent on despoiling. They will without compunction despatch him to eternity after taking their prey. At every impulse of thought or imagination to ward off fear or obtain pleasure, their minds open up to them some way of deception or a means of force. In these ways, plunder displaces free exchange and contention contentment. Fraud or violence become the arbiters of human conduct.

But human cupidity is not limited to rivalry over bodily pleasures and the conflicts of greed in pursuit of supposed ends —if there are any ends to human acquisitiveness. On the contrary. Man is a being with spiritual ambitions also, one of the most significant of which is the desire to be well thought of by others with whom society brings him into relation, through its whole reaches. This appetite for praise can almost over-master all other passions: there is quite unmatched fascination in the drive to satisfy it. It is in fact one of the best factors in the attainment of the virtues, and stabilizing inter-personal and international relations—if only it be exercised in the proper way. But, as we have said in an earlier allusion, it has like other

Man's Need of Prophetic Mission

moral factors been perverted and depraved, because of the disparities in human powers of mind and of resolution. Many have formed the idea of acquiring high repute among men by intimidating and disquieting peaceable folk to gain the tribute of awed fear, not the respect of reverence.

Is it possible that any community, founding its order and depending for its perpetuation on mutual help and reliance, could exist in such a state of things? Would not all the factors passed under review in the foregoing mean that it would disintegrate and disappear? There can be no doubt that survival on these terms would be impossible. Undoubtedly the human species must have love, or an effective equivalent, if it is to ensure its perpetuation.

Some perceptive minds have, at different times, taken refuge in the concept of justice. They have taken the view, along with some of the mystical thinkers who gave it eloquent expression, that justice can fill the role of love. The observation, indeed, has its point. But who is to lay down the rules of justice and bring about their general observance? It is said that reason will achieve this. Just as thought, memory and imagination were the source of the trouble, so they could likewise be the means to happiness and the haven of tranquillity. We have noted that moderation of mind, breadth of knowledge, the power of reason and strength of judgement have enabled many to get beyond enveloping passions and illusory fears and with reverence to acknowledge every right for what it is and to discriminate between the pleasure that is transitory and the benefit that abides. There have been those in every nation who have laid down the principles of virtue and made clear the nature of evil, distinguishing between human actions fraught with immediate pleasure and evil sequence—and so to be avoided—and those which are perhaps hard to bear but have joy in their end and are thus to be pursued. Nor have these champions of justice lacked among them those who in their call to men suffered death or loss. There have been martyrs among them who faithfully summoned their people to the true security of their institutions. These are the thinkers who lay down the principles of justice. Men in authority have the onus of bringing the masses into a true recognition of them, so that human affairs may proceed rightly.

It might seem that this position is a valid one. Yet does the human story provide a record, or human patterns sustain the supposition, of the whole or the majority of mankind being subject to the ideas of the wise, for the sole and simple reason that they are sound? Is it adequately persuasive for one of the intelligentsia to tell a community, a people, or a nation, that they are in error and that he has the right way and summons them to it? Even if he brought corroborating evidence clearer than daylight and plainer than the fact of life being necessary to survival, would they respond? Indeed not. History gives no warrant for such a hope; nor does human nature bear it out. We have earlier insisted that human troubles arise from the discrepancies between men in intelligence, while at the same time they claim to have an equality of ability and to be of essentially comparable quality. In fact, however, the bulk of men do not know the difference between the worthy and the ignorant. He who does not have your degree of intelligence obviously will not share your sense of what is worthy. Mere rational proof does not obviate conflict nor bring about a settled concord. It may be that the very disciples of the law of reason will pretend to a higher status than those who enjoined it, leading people into the path of their passions and so to destroying the sanctity of reason itself, and with it the whole edifice and the intention within it.

Added to all the foregoing in the conflicts of thought and appetite, is another factor in the shape of a feeling instinctive to man and inexorably strong, namely the inward sense in every one, however high-minded and mentally vigorous, however dull-witted and feeble, that he is subject to some force greater than his own and that of his stronger fellows around him. This force has an over-mastering quality and disposes both of him and his, in a manner that human experience has never fathomed and mere human volition cannot match.

Every one feels the impulse to know what this great force is and seeks to do so, from time to time, by sense or by reason. There is no way to track it down, save the properly human way of study. So each man takes up the pursuit, with thought as the pioneer. Some have had the search lead them to the animal kingdom with its great potential for good and for ill. Others have sought its likeness in the stars: others see it concealed in trees and rocks: others again have divinized it in the hints of special powers belonging to diverse species, and emerging in particular members, as varied as they are numerous.

But whenever feelings have been refined and thinking has grown more subtle and awareness more pentrating, these ideas have been transcended, with comparably finer consequences. Among the espousers of such worthier thoughts have been some who attained to the knowledge of this surpassing power and came to identify it with the necessarily existing Being, though many aspects of Almightiness remained veiled to them and they were still prone to confusion. Nor did they have a sufficiently powerful quality to carry their people along with them, so that contradictory theories remained current and true guidance was rarely followed.

Men were of one mind about the need to submit to the higher power beyond their attaining. But they differed sharply in their understanding of what their conscience bade them obey and there were consequent divergencies of a deeply disruptive character. These created cleavages as wide as those with which men's passion bedevilled the rival views on pleasure and pain.

Man has a natural propensity for community. But unlike bees and ants, for example, he has not been granted the instinctive faculty for what community requires. Rather, as we have seen, he has ideas of his own and follows these. Though he has an awareness of an all-powerful Being and an urge, in spite of himself, to acknowledge it, yet he does not enjoy the knowledge of the essence and attributes thereof. Instead, he is left wandering in the loose ends of learning, in a tumult of thoughts that land him only in indecision and confusion, with dire consequences for himself and his community. Must we then ask whether man is in worse case, with his frustrations and limitations, than the lowest of the animals in the scale of existence? Indeed, it would be so, were it not for that by which the wise creator has countered his frailty.

Man is a strange and wonderful being. By force of intellect he climbs to the highest realms of Divine lordship. His thought attains the utmost reaches of Divine power. He pits his strength against the very forces of the universe which defy him. Yet he is cut down to size and falls into the most abject abasement when he is confronted with something he cannot get to the bottom of or explain. Though all men everywhere are familiar enough with man as he is, only the illuminated (*al-mustabṣirūn*) have the clue.

It is in fact this very frailty which has led man to truth. Out of this very humiliation, he is manuducted into honour and well-being. For the gracious giver of all has brought into perfect climax for the entirety of mankind what His wisdom necessitated in that peculiarly human condition and in the privation we know as individuals. Just as He has granted to each person the reason and sense-perception with which to search out items of food and clothe his nakedness and protect himself from heat and cold, so has He granted to the whole of mankind as one that much more urgent need that has to do with his survival and with his immunity from the calamities of distress and the preservation of the communal order in which his true being lies. God has bestowed on man a gift which in truth takes up the role of love, re-establishing it in men's souls in their loveless wasteland. It is a gift which does not contravene man's pattern under God or the grounds of his being in teaching and right guidance. Yet it comes to man, nevertheless, just where he is most wanting and requires humility and submission. From among men themselves God has raised up guides and mentors whom He has distinguished with unique qualities of soul, attesting them with remarkable signs well calculated to convince or to forestall the predilections of reason. So the pretentious learn to submit and the refractory are humbled. The intelligent find their reason brought up sharp and so back into a true course, while the ignorant are overwhelmed and turn away from their deceits.

By Divine command, these guides knock loudly upon our hearts' doors and amaze our souls by the splendour of the Divine signs. They invest the mind like a citadel that finds no option but to surrender. Kings and subjects, princes and paupers, learned and ignorant, the élite and the rest—all alike are equal in status before the message of the prophets. To submit to them is more like a necessity than a studious option of will.

Man's Need of Prophetic Mission

They teach men what God has ordered for their good in mortal life and beyond, and the things He wills them to know of His essence and the perfection of His attributes. These are the prophets, the messengers of God, whose mission fulfills the very being of man and constitutes one of his deepest needs as meant for eternity. What reason is to the individual person, the prophets are to mankind—a mercy from God, 'so that men might have no plea against God after the coming of His messengers' (Surah 4.165). We will come shortly in greater detail to their office under God.

Chapter 9

THE POSSIBILITY OF RELEVATION

Discussion of the possibility of revelation must be preceded by definition of the term and what it is intended to signify. We know the thing which transpires from an action by reference to the action itself, rather than by the effect the mere word has in our minds. We remember from language what accords with such action. Some one will say: 'You revealed to so and so . . .' meaning that you spoke to him about something you kept hidden from others. *Al-Waḥy* is the verbal noun from that verb. Some written thing, the message you addressed to your other party to bring him information, may also be so termed. The dominant meaning of 'revelation' has come to be what has been addressed to the prophets from God. It is also said that 'revelation' is informing in secret, and the thing revealed is sometimes what is meant. In the sacred law, 'revelation' is known as God's disclosure to one of the prophets by and according to His legislative decree. For our purposes we define it as the knowledge a man finds within himself with the utter assurance that it has come from God, by or without an intermediary. The former may be by a voice identifiable by hearing, or without a voice. The difference between *Waḥy* and *Ilhām*, or inspiration, lies in the fact that inspiration is a sensation of which man is inwardly aware, and is impelled by, without sensing whence it came. It may be likened to the consciousness of thirst, or hunger, of grief or delight.

If it be asked whether the awareness we call *Waḥy* can in fact take place, and with it the disclosure of things to do with human welfare that are hidden from the mass of men, to those whom God particularly chooses for this end, as well as its ready comprehension by the mind—I reply that I see no reason why this should be a difficult matter to apprehend, except for the wilfully

The Possibility of Revelation

obdurate. Doubtless all times and peoples afford examples of those whom heedlessness and lack of knowledge exclude from the harbours of conviction. Such indeed fall into abysmal doubts over everything that does not come within their five senses. Or, as we have seen earlier, they even question the evidence of these, falling thus, it would seem, lower even than the animals. They neglect the mind, its tasks and secrets, perversely preferring a kind of liberation in this way from the bonds of obligations and restraints—even the conventions of modesty and the sense of what is fitting, to the point of animality rather than humanity. When religion or prophecy addresses people of this ilk, and there is no escape hatch into heedlessness, they will defend themselves by pleading liberty of view as their right. They will evade the issue with their fingers in their ears, lest the evidence should confuse their minds, and they be duty-bound to acknowledge the doctrine and follow the sacred law, so forfeiting the pleasures they love and enjoy. Such are in the grip of a soul-disease, which only knowledge, by God's will, can heal.

So I say, what is there impossible in the belief in revelation, in the disclosure to a particular prophet of what is not known to others, and that without conscious thinking or deductive reasoning, but by the giver of thought, the bestower of perception, under the Divine protection and distinguishing favour?

There is ample evidence that intelligence varies widely in degree. The lowest only remotely apprehend what the wisest know. The disparity arises not merely from unequal instruction but also from basic differences in capacity which the will or acquisition of the person cannot effect. What requires reflective study on the part of some minds is undoubtedly at once evident to finer intelligence. These degrees of intelligence extend very far. Men of resolution and noble mind will readily seek and find what to inferior souls remains far and inaccessible, a thing they deny at the outset and greet with amazement at the end. In turn, however, these lesser minds will get used to the consequences that amazed them and start to treat them as familiar and incontrovertible, to the point where they will be round with any one who gainsays them, in adopting what was once their own incredulity. A few of this type of people may still be found in all nations even today.

If it be allowed—as in truth it must—that the foregoing premises are sound, it would be weak-minded and perverse not to acknowledge that there are among men those of such pure quality of soul and inward disposition, as to be joined with the highest realms by virtue of a Divine abundance of grace by which they attain the utmost human eminence. These see the things of God as if by natural vision, such as others could reach neither by reason nor sense, even with the aid of proof and demonstration. From God, the all-knowing and all wise, they learn more clearly than any of us do from instructors in doctrine. What they have been taught, they teach, and call men to what they have been enjoined to bring to them. This is the way God works in every people and time, as He sees the need. By His mercy, He manifests His chosen and protected messengers to bring to all the imperatives that belong with their well-being, tempering the human fibre to its strongest and ensuring that the tokens He has ordained for their guidance will effectuate their purpose of human blessedness. The message and mission are then sealed and the door of prophethood closed, as will appear in our exposition of Muḥammad, the peace and blessing of God be upon him.

If we are really aware of ourselves, we will find nothing impossible in the existence of angelic beings—the revered angels—and their appearing to men of this noble quality. Of old and of late science has assured us that there are in existence beings more subtle than material things, albeit concealed from us. Is there anything to forbid the Divine knowledge from radiating within this subtle immateriality and the souls of the prophets from perceiving it? Would not dependable word of that occurring constrain in us a full submission to its authenticity?

As for the likeness of a voice speaking and the visible shapes of those spirits in the experience of those who have the prophetic vocation, even those who contest the whole thing concede something very like it, in the state of sufferers from certain diseases—a claim they explicitly make. It is agreed that here some mental forms take actual shape in their imagination and are even sensibly experienced. The sick man in his own words 'sees' and 'hears': indeed he struggles and wrestles, though in actuality there is nothing of that. For the representation is only

The Possibility of Revelation

in mental pictures and has no ground save in the man himself. Now if this kind of thing happens in an accidental circumstance affecting the brain, why should it be impossible that intelligible truths take shape in noble souls, when they are abstracted from the realm of sense and are caught into Paradise? Will not this experience be entirely congruent with their true intelligence, as those with unique and peculiar qualities, not shared by other mortals? We must necessarily assume that the association of soul and body in their case is other than what obtains with the rest of men. That is all we can say. It is a readily acceptable, indeed an imperative, conclusion, given their status, for which the familiar world has no parallel. It is, of course, their uniqueness which more than anything else constitutes the proof of their message. Their integrity and the authenticity of their words lie in the healing of the sicknesses of men by their remedies. Frailty of purpose and of mind is transformed to strength among the peoples who give them heed. It is manifestly impossible that health should issue from the sick or that the disordered mind should guide into the path of ordered peace.

The prophetic status is one thing. On a lower level are the men of high soul and intellectual excellence—the inner circle of the knowers (*al 'urafā'*) who rejoice to be the helpers of the prophets and faithful retainers of their law and message. Many of them come near to the prophets in a communion of kinship and spirit, and in some conditions they have access in part to the ultimate mysteries and true insights into the visionary world that are undeniable and find fulfilment in the actual. They are thus able the more readily to substantiate prophetic experience. He who has tasted knows, and he who has not entered goes astray. Only by inclusion is there not exclusion. It is the manifestly good consequence of their message which gives evidence of their veracity and the fact that in their actions they never flout the laws of their prophets. They are pure from the things that any sound intelligence and a proper sense of value would repudiate. It is the shining truth speaking in their innermost hearts which constrains them to summon all who will to its benison and to re-animate the special few. There are of course some in the world who make idle pretension to be saints: but their deception is quickly revealed. They and the victims of their deceit come to a miserable end. Their effects are always evil, misguiding men's minds and corrupting their manners. The nation that suffers them falls into decline, unless God in His goodness stays them in their course. Their words are like an uprooted tree that has no bond with the ground. They falsely conceal the truth about themselves.

Those who deny the reality of prophethood and the prophets' insights and those who are assured of the feasibility of their message and its actuality are separated only by a veil—the veil of habit. It is this which so often conceals from men's minds the realisation of the things with which they are thoroughly familiar.

Chapter 10

REVELATION AND MISSION IN THEIR ACTUALITY

The proof of the message of a prophet and the truth of what he delivers from his Lord is evident before the eye-witness who sees him as he is and beholds the clear signs that God grants. This verification by actual sight dispenses with other evidence, as earlier argued in the section on prophetic mission. However, in the case of those who do not belong to the prophet's time and place, the proof lies in successive testimony. The elaboration of this is another branch of knowledge. The narration of information about a seen-event on the part of a community of whom it is impossible to think that they conspired to deceive, and supported by the sign, powerfully assures man of the certainty of its content. One might cite information about the existence of Mecca or about China having a capital called Peking. Such statements are exempt from the suspicion of calculated deception, since their content is thoroughly open to known tests and offers no grounds for misgiving. Number is the decisive element in all this and the disinterestedness of the narrator.

There is no question among the intelligent that this kind of information brings assured conviction. But there is dispute about the considerations that have to do with the informant. The story of some of the prophets is related to us exhaustively with unbroken attestation—among them Abraham, Moses and Jesus. We learn of them that they were not the greatest in power or wealth, of the people to whom they were sent. No one had any particular concern for their instruction in the things they were to present for men's acceptance. The sum of it simply is that they were not of the low, despicable kind that men avoid. Yet despite the fact that temporal authority was in other hands, which disposed also of the wealth and had dominance by dint of superior learning, they fulfilled their mission to call men to God, and that in spite of kings and their armies. Their voice shook the monarchs on their thrones. They claimed to inform men of the law which the creator of the heavens and the earth had willed for them, verifying it with proofs which reduced the opposition to contempt. They thus established their laws in the world and planted them in the instincts of the heart. The nations found their good in their obedience.

As long as they observed these laws the peoples found power with them and happy was their case. But when they abandoned or confused them, they were overtaken by weakness and distress. This fact, coupled with the evidences they performed when challenged, makes it quite irrational to think that they were lying in what they said on God's behalf, and in their claims to have been inspired by Him in their law-giving. For he who does not believe his own words has no abiding impact on other men's minds. The false man cannot last, except where people are negligent, just as noxious weeds only grow in the good earth when it is uncared for. Given the caring hand of the farmer, fertility and good growth will oust the weeds. The religions of the prophets have performed in this human world the role which God willed and ordered for them, as He did for the rest of His means and agencies—and that despite much resistance, well-armed with power and authority. It is impossible that their work could have been reared and sustained in trickery and deceit. Even through the accretions of the innovators this essential glory shines perpetually. It is of this we now speak.

As for the rest of the messengers on whom it is incumbent we believe, the evidences confirming the message of Muḥammad our Prophet will suffice for them also. He has informed us of their mission and his deliverances are trustworthy. We shall take up the mission of our Prophet for exposition in a separate chapter.

THE ROLE OF THE MESSENGERS OF GOD

What we have earlier said about the messengers being to the nations what reason is to the person illuminates the need of the Islamic world for those messengers. Their mission is one of the

Revelation and Mission in their Actuality 101

needs of the human mind which in mercy the wise creator has ordained should be met and one of the acts of grace by which the bestower of all being has favoured man uniquely among His creatures. It is a spiritual need. Those aspects which do bear on the realm of the senses are simply for the purpose of cleansing the soul from the defilement of erring passions or for the reforming of its faculties to bring about happiness in this life and the next.

Only in terms of general exhortation and precepts of moderation does the prophetic mission bear upon the business of work-a-day life and upon men's acquisitive skills and the spreading ventures of their minds into the secrets of science. Prophets are only concerned to insist that the underlying condition of all such activity is that it occasion no doubt as to the universe having one God, who is almighty, omniscient, wise, with all the attributes which proof has established to be believed of Him. Their message brooks no denial of the truth that all beings have equality before Him as His creatures and the work of His power, differentiated as they are by the qualities of perfection with which some of them are favoured. The prophets also require that no evil, either to himself, his estate or his possessions, be incurred by any one for those activities, unless it be by virtue of some proper factor relating to the general order of the nation and within the approval of the sacred law.

The prophets guide the mind to the knowledge of God and what must be known of His attributes, as well as the limits we are obliged to observe in the pursuit of such knowledge—though this must be in such wise as not to shake man's confidence or deprive him of his assurance about reason as a God-given power. The prophets bring into one consensus creation's confession of one, undivided God. They clear of impediments the way of man to God and arouse men's souls to utter dependence upon Him in all things. They remind men of His greatness, laying down the different times of worship so that the forgetful may remember and as a constant chastening for the fearful to fortify their weakness, as well as to intensify the assurance of the strong in faith.

They show to men the discordancies in their minds and desires, over their interests and pleasures, applying to all such contentions the decisive commandment of God. By their message from Him they foster the common good without thereby impairing private interests.

They restore men to fellowship and reveal to them the secret of love as the inclusive principle of human community, laying upon them the task of training their souls to dwell with love as their hearts' native land, wherein each learns to preserve every other's right while not neglecting his own. They teach men to keep their demands in proper check, the strong helping the weak and the rich the poor within society, with the true guiding the erring and the learned teaching the ignorant.

By Divine authority they set for men the general limits to which they may readily relate all their actions. Among these are the sanctity of human life, save in those cases where the right to take it is laid down, the duty to refrain from taking what is another's except where the right to do so explicitly exists, the sanctity of sexual relations and what is allowed and what forbidden in respect of marriage. They enjoin them also to train themselves in the exercise of the virtue of honesty, fidelity, integrity, steadfastness to pledges, mercy toward the weak, fearlessness of counsel to the mighty and the acknowledgement without exception of the rights of every creature.

They also urge men to turn their appetite for transitory pleasures into the search after worthy desires, employing therein, after God's command and in careful balance, the double appeal both to yearning and to fear, with exhortations both glad and grave.

They clarify, too, the deeds which merit the Divine pleasure and incur the Divine wrath. Through all their words runs the theme of the celestial world and all the recompense of God which God has pledged to those who observe His precepts, perform His commands and steer clear of complicity in the forbidden.

They teach men such tidings of the eternal realms as God has willed for His servants to know. To fathom these is more than mind can compass: but their reality is readily confessed.

Thus the souls of men find rest and refreshment: the afflicted find shelter in patience, in hope of ample reward or the 'well done' of their Lord. And thus the greatest problem of human

Revelation and Mission in their Actuality   103

society, which to this day the minds of men have restlessly toiled to solve, finds resolution.

It does not belong to the office of the messengers to be instructors and teachers of crafts. They do not deal with the lessons of history nor with the analysis of astronomical worlds and the diverse theories of stars in their courses. Outside their province are the storehouses of the earth, the dimensions of the world's length and breadth, the sciences that study plants in their growth and animals in their quest to survive. All of these, and more, belong with the relevant branches of learning and have been the arena of much eager rivalry over their detailed investigation. These things belong wholly with the means to material acquisition and well-being and are within those gifts of comprehension whereby God has willed that men be directed. Those who pursue these sciences increase in prosperity but short-comers incur only trouble. Only gradually does man attain to perfection—so runs the Divine principle. The prophetic laws are to promote endeavour along this path, in a general sense, and to sustain man in the attainment of the high dignity that God has promised to human nature.

There are in the words of the prophets references to some of the above mentioned topics, like the movements in the heavens and the fashion of the earth. These, however, intend only to direct attention to the creator's wisdom or to depth in the apprehension of His mysteries and marvels. The prophetic language in addressing their peoples must not be above their heads or otherwise the Divine wisdom in their mission will be in vain. For this reason expressions directed originally to the common people may contain a depth of meaning requiring elucidation and exposition among the special few. A long time is necessary for the esoteric meaning to become understandable among the masses. This element, however, is the least part of what the prophets had to say.

At all events, religion must not be made into a barrier, separating men's spirits from God-given abilities in the knowledge of the truths of the contingent world as far as in them lies. Rather, religion must promote this very search, demanding respect for evidence and enjoining the utmost possible devotion and endeavour through all the worlds of knowledge—and all within the true proportions of the goal, holding fast the while to sound itself. Any who assert the contrary do not know what religion is and do despite to it which the Lord of the worlds will not forgive.

A WELL-KNOWN OBJECTION

But it will be said that if the mission of the prophets is an essential need of mankind for the perfecting of their social order and as a way to well-being in both worlds, then why on earth is mankind still in such a troubled state? Men are far from being happy. There are discords, not concord. They fight against each other instead of winning common victories. There is mutual recrimination instead of mutual help. Each takes up a belligerent attitude, awaiting the favourable moment. Injustice fills men's thoughts and greed their souls. The partisans of each religion make their belief a ground of contention against those who hold differently, leading to new enmities and rancours, more bitter than those which attend the clash of general interests and gain. The people of one religion are sundered by schism into diversified schools of interpretation. Dogmas are the occasion of dog-fights, and in the dust of controversy evils break out and passions engender seditions, and blood flows. Force takes over, instead of truth and religion becomes a shambles with the strong against the weak. What then is this thing religion, which claims to be the great unifier, the apostle of love? What is there to these proud claims? Ponder the actual picture —discord and hatred at their very worst.

We say in reply: Yes! indeed. The picture is true. But the reason lies in the fact that after the time of the prophets and the passing of their régime, religion fell into the hands of those who quite failed to understand it, or lapsed into extremism, or else they did not sincerely love it at all. Or if they had a real love, their minds were inadequate for its full implementation according to the prophets or the best of their followers. Let the questioner say. Is there a single prophet who failed to bring his nation the utmost good and to do so with an all embracing fulness? Is there one whose religion fell short of any need of his people, whether as a community or as individuals?

Revelation and Mission in their Actuality

I assume that no one will contest my view that the vast majority of people, indeed all but a very few, fail to understand the philosophy of Plato and have no competence of thought for the logic of Aristotle. Indeed, if an exponent were to put it to them in the clearest possible terms, choosing the themes of readiest comprehension, they would have only an inconsequential reaction, confined to their imaginations alone and without any efficacy for their conduct or edification. Consider people of this sort as they truly are, caught in the flux of passions. Suppose yourself a preacher whose job it is to allay their evil case, itself the sad entail of their strife. What would be your way of attacking the problem set by their unbridled desires? How would you propose to bring some sort of order and sanity into them?

It is obvious that you would hardly find the clue in simply showing the evil consequences that follow on indulgence, or the benefits of purposeful desire, and the like. For even the intellectual élite only attain to these things after long reflection. Rather you would find the surest and most effective way in making their conscience responsive to the mystery of that authority which surrounds them on all sides—monitor of the Divine power, from whom every gift derives. For that Divine viceroy masters their innermost thoughts and knows the soul within. It possesses all their ways. Drive towards your point with examples close to their familiar thoughts and relate the stories that edify and impress from the resources of whatever religion it is. Use the noble precedents of the early believers with their fine moral force. Quicken men with the mention of God's pleasure in the upright and His wrath against those who throw off the rein. By such an approach men's hearts may become submissive, even with tears. Wrath may be allayed and passion stayed. The hearer may understand only one thought in all this, namely the idea of pleasing God and His chosen worshippers by obedience, and of incurring their wrath by his recalcitrance. So it has been seen in the human condition, both of old and in these days. He who denies it is not belonging with humanity.

How often have we heard of tears and sighs and humbled hearts at the preaching of religion? But have you heard the like from the appeals of moralists or political leaders? When have we heard tell of a group of men who have come into good, active good, merely by the argument of its being beneficial to society or to a few? When has evil been eliminated simply by appeal to the fact that it is harmful and deleterious in its effects? Such things do not happen in history. Nor do they square with human nature. The ground of moral character is in beliefs and traditions and these can be built only on religion. The religious factor is, therefore, the most powerful of all, in respect both of public and of private ethics. It exercises an authority over men's souls superior to that of reason, despite man's uniquely rational powers.

We have observed that the prophets are to the corporate and social what reason is to the personal. It may be likened to the role of a sign denoting the passable road. We can go further and say that it is the faculty which hears and sees. Does not the viewer distinguish between the beautiful and the unworthy, between the easy path and the crooked, rugged ones? Even so, he may make an evil use of the powers of sight he possesses, and fall into a pit and perish, with two sound eyes in his head, through heedlessness, that is, or negligence and inattention, or again through obstinacy. Bring a thousand proofs to reason and sense, as to the evil potential of some action or other, and the evil man who wants it will counter the very evidence he admits with other apparent proofs and go madly for the hateful thing in the stubborness of his passion. One should not, however, let these examples detract from the competence of mind and of sense in their proper form and field. The messengers, then, are the signs God has given to guide men in the way of salvation. Those who have accepted the guidance have come to happiness. Those who have misunderstood or fallen away from their light have come to a bitter end. Religion is a guide. But human weakness impedes those who are called to take its guidance to themselves. Yet that weakness does not disqualify the perfection of religion, nor yet man's urgent need for it. 'God leads some astray and others He enlightens: but only the evil-doers does He mislead.' (Surah 2.26.)

Religion is the haunt of peaceableness and the refuge of tranquillity. It makes each man content with his lot. It spurs the doer to that persistence which will carry him through, and by religion men learn submission to the general principles that obtain in their existence. It teaches men to look up to their superiors in knowledge and virtue, though they may be inferior in wealth and reputation—and all in conformity to the Divine precepts.

Religion is more like an instinctive, spontaneous impulse of nature than calculated claims on the will. It is one of the most powerful forces in man, and as other forces are it is vulnerable from without. When attacks are made upon it, such as the one we are here discussing, the responsibility rests with its adherents, upon those who have undertaken the duty of its propagation, the recognised custodians and guardians of its principles. In their task of bringing it home to men's hearts, they can only be conformed to its guidance, return to its pure, primal origins and rid it of heretical accretion. Then its authority will come again and even the blind will recognise its wisdom.

It may possibly be said that this comparison between reason and religion involves some disparagement of the former in matters of faith. Some espouse this very notion arguing that faith is founded on pure submission and is quite discontinuous with rational investigation of the contents of religion, whether it be doctrines affirmed or directives enjoined. We reply: if that claim were to be allowed, religion would not be a means whereby man could be guided. As already affirmed, mind alone does not suffice to attain the condition in which the well-being of humankind resides. It needs a Divine guide. Animals, for example, cannot solely rely on sight among their senses but must use hearing also. Religion is a general 'sense' by which to discover the things that elude reason among the means to happiness. Mind is authoritative for the knowledge of this faculty and its exercise in its proper field. Mind submits to the doctrines and rules of conduct that religion discloses.

How then can reason be denied its right, being, as it is, the scrutineer of evidences so as to reach the truth within them and know that it is Divinely given? Having, however, once recognised the mission of a prophet, reason is obliged to acknowledge all that he brings, even though unable to attain the essential meaning within it or penetrate its full truth. Yet this obligation does not involve reason in accepting rational impossibilities such as two incompatibles or opposites together at the same time and point. For prophecies are immune from bringing such follies. But if there comes something which appears contradictory reason must believe that the apparent is not the intended sense. It is then free to seek the true sense by reference to the rest of the prophet's message in whom the ambiguity occurred, or to fall back upon God and His omniscience. There have been those among our forebears who have chosen to do either one or the other.

Chapter 11

THE MISSION AND MESSAGE OF MUḤAMMAD

It is not intended in these few brief pages to treat the history of the nations in general and the Arabs in particular at the time of Muḥammad's mission, or to show how the world and its peoples were in urgent need of a clarion call to shake the thrones of kings and challenge the foundations of their tyranny and bring down their pretensions from high heaven to ponder the condition of their wretched subjects. We do not linger here on the need of mankind for a fire from heaven, a fire of truth to descend upon the rank undergrowth of vanities strangling the works of reason, or their need for some eloquent cry to arouse the negligent, recover the dazed and awaken the oppressed to the fact that they were no less human than their tyrannical oppressors, their erring guides and treacherous leaders—men's need, in sum, for direction on the road of the Divine will. 'We have guided him in the way,' (Surah 76.3) that therein man might rightly come to his full stature and reach the things prepared for him both here and hereafter. We must be content to borrow from this history a single theme agreed by historians of that period and familiar enough to those who ponder it carefully and with open mind.

The two major empires of the world, Persia in the east and Byzantium in the west, were in continual conflict and war—costly in blood, in exhaustion of power and in material destruction, and all—under darkening shadows of bitter hatred. There was unparalleled opulence and arrogance, luxurious living and indulgence in many forms, alike in royal palaces and among amirs, sultans and religious leaders on either side. Their greed knew no bounds. Taxes were extortionate and excise duties so excessive that they became more than the population could bear, depriving the people of the due fruits of their labours. Those who had the power used it to snatch from them the possessions of the poor, while the clever schemed to steal from the foolish. And in consequence these nations fell victims to the multiplied evils of poverty, degradation, fear and turmoil. Neither soul nor property were secure.

The common people were left with no more spirit in them by the arbitrary actions of their rulers and were reduced to puppets like those behind a show curtain which the spectator thinks to be moving freely. Personal independence was filched away. Some even came to thinking they were created only for this servitude to their overlords, to do their every pleasure like dumb beasts. The rulers lapsed from their beliefs and were carried away by their appetites, wreaking nothing of truth and justice and retaining in the general atrophy of their intellectual powers only a perverted ability to think evil. Their incessant fear was lest the Divine light which belongs with human nature should break through into their subjects' hearts and pierce the veil over their minds and show them the way of mass revolt against the tyrant few. For that reason, kings and rulers were careful to spread clouds of illusion, shrouding the common folk with dark superstitions and vain follies, aggravating their ignorance and, by the utter eclipse of reason, binding them to their bidding like helpless slaves. The religious leaders affirmed in its name that religion was the enemy of reason and all its reflective works, unless tied exclusively to commentary on sacred texts. Paganism was an unfailing source, a never depleted stock, from which they could draw to perpetuate their popular hold.

This was how those peoples were in their cultural and material life—oppressed slaves sunk in blind ignorance. There were a few exceptions among those with whom survived something of the wisdom of the past and of the earlier laws still lingering in their minds. For such the present was utterly detestable, but the past they only dimly glimpsed.

Doubt was rampant about the very principles and implications of belief, through distortion and contradiction in their meaning and character. The foul was taken for pure, and greed

The Mission and Message of Muhammad

for temperance. Immorality reigned where peace and integrity should have been. Paying scant attention to the real causes, men readily attributed to religion the source of their decadence. Unrest spread its sway over all thinking. Reason and the sacred law alike were a prey to disruptive forces and advocates of anarchism and materialism raised their heads on many sides, further to aggravate the sorry condition of things.

The Arab nation consisted of various tribes, sundered by conflicts and enslaved by passions. Each tribe gloried in wars with its neighbour, capturing the women folk, killing the chieftains and pillaging the land. Greed inspired these perpetual battles. With the decay of belief went every sort of evil. So low did the Arabs' intelligence sink that they even made sugar idols and worshipped them, and ate them when they were hungry. In their helpless degradation they slew their girl children to be rid of the disgrace of them or to be free of the burden of keeping them alive. Chastity had no worth in their eyes, so far were they gone in moral turpitude. In a word, all the bonds of the social order in every people and community were slackened and dissolved.

Was it not then of God's mercy on these peoples that He brought them to heel by one of their own number in whom He inspired His message, bestowing on him His care and enabling him to dispel these dark distresses hanging over all people? It was indeed God's mercy. For He controls all, from beginning to end.

On the night of Rabī'a al-Awwal 12, in the year of the elephant, April 20, AD 571, Muḥammad ibn 'Abdallāh ibn 'Abd al-Muṭṭalib ibn Hāshim, the Quraishī, was born in Mecca. He was a posthumous child. When his father died before his birth he left only five camels, a few sheep and a female slave—perhaps even less than that. In his sixth year, Muḥammad lost his mother also and 'Abd al-Muṭṭalib, his grandfather, took him into his care. But after two years again, he died and then Abū Ṭālib, his uncle, became his guardian. Despite his poverty with hardly enough resources for his immediate family, Abū Ṭālib was energetic and kindly. Muḥammad was reared among his cousins and the boys of the tribe, different only in his being orphaned of both parents and by the fact of a poverty that afflicted alike both ward and guardian. He had no tutor for his education, no teacher to care for his instruction. His contemporaries had grown up in the days of ignorance and his companions were sworn idolaters. He was among the patrons and servants of images: his own relatives shared in the heathen cult. Nevertheless he grew into a fine character, both morally and mentally, so that he became known among the people of Mecca in his youth as Al-Amīn, the trustworthy. Thus he had a Divine good-breeding, quite unusual among poor orphans, the more so when his mentors were poor also. He came to a ripe maturity, nobly acknowledging the Divine unity among a people who were deprived and depraved and idolatrous. He was quiet among dissidents, of sound belief among the deluded, with an innate goodness among a people in ignorance, ill-discipline and delusion.

A poor and illiterate orphan such as he would normally take his character from the environment of his infancy and youth, his mind being influenced by what he heard around him, and especially from his relatives and immediate family—the more so as he had neither book to guide nor teacher to arouse, nor aid in making his resolutions active. Had things gone in the way one would expect, Muḥammad would have adopted their beliefs and opinions, at least until he came to mature manhood and had occasion for thought and reflection such as might enable him to turn and repudiate their errors once the evidence against them had come home to him. This indeed happened with one or two persons about that time. But it was not thus with the Prophet. From his earliest years, Muḥammad found a deep revulsion from paganism. Purity of belief was his from the outset and excellence of character, as the Qur'ān says: 'Did He not find you wandering and guide you?' (Surah 93.7). We do not understand from this that he was involved in idolatry before being guided to the unity, or that he trod improper ways before his pre-eminent stature. God forbid: that would be manifest falsehood. The 'wandering' refers to the perplexity in the hearts of the sincere in their yearning for other men's salvation and their search for the way to rescue the perishing and direct the erring. God indeed led His Prophet to that goal he had in his vision, through the sense of being chosen for His mission, his calling from all creation to enunciate the Divine law.

The Mission and Message of Muḥammad   113

Certain resources came his way to meet his needs. 'And with their increase his manner of life could readily have become luxurious,'—thanks to his work for Khadījah in merchandising and her subsequent choice of him as a husband. What accrued to him from the profits of his work was enough to enable a manner of life equal to that of the greatest of his people. But the world had no enticements for him, nor did its luxuries deceive. He eschewed the way of those who used such wealth to gratify their desires. As he grew in years, Muḥammad came more and more to love solitude away from society and the familiar world, alone with his thoughts and reflections. He felt the need for devotion and to take refuge in God, with quiet entreaty, to find the solution of his great pre-occupation—the salvation of his people and of the world from the evil in whose grip it lay. He sought the rending of the veil from the world to which Divine inspiration urged him, that the holy light might come radiantly upon him, with the descent of revelation from on high. There is no place here to enter more fully into this.

There was no king among his fathers, for him to reclaim a long lost kingdom. His own people, moreover, were quite adverse to authority and ranks of power. They were happy enough with their custodianship of the sacred place. A story of his grandfather, 'Abd al-Muṭṭalib and the advance of the Ethiopian, Abraha, against the city, well illustrates both aspects of the Meccans. Abraha came for revenge on the Arabs by destroying their sanctuary, the hallowed house and centre of pilgrimage, the high seat of their deities, and the supreme point of Quraishī pride among their people. Some of Abraha's army, in their advance, rounded up a number of camels including two hundred belonging to 'Abd al-Muṭṭalib. He went out with some Quraishī to meet the king, who received him and enquired his errand. He replied that he wanted his two hundred camels restored. The king rebuked him for such a mean request when so large issues were at stake. To which 'Abd al-Muṭṭalib replied that he was the master of the camels. The sacred house had its own Lord to protect it.

To this degree were they ready to leave all things with God— and 'Abd al-Muṭṭalib was a person of eminence in Quraishī affairs. How then could Muḥammad, poor as he was, and no

H

more than a middle class citizen, have any pretensions to authority or claims to power. He had neither property nor status, nor army, nor supporters. He had no bent for poetry, no special competence in letters, no reputation for public speaking. He was quite devoid of the capacities needed to seize a position of popular influence or attain to special status.

What was it which gave him pre-eminence over men and set him above their level, which gave him his extra-ordinary intensity of purpose that he should be chosen to lead the nations, to dispel their sorrows and even to breathe life into their decayed society?

In answer, we must say that it was the awareness God gave him of the need of the world for the recovery of true belief, for the reform of its corrupted morals and manners. It was the inward sense, nothing less, of the wind of Divine compassion bearing him into action and victory, and on to the final goal of his hope before death's own finality overtook him. It was none other than the Divine revelation, lightening the way before him and like a captain and a warrior leading him in its heavenly authenticity. See him rise up single-handed and alone to call all people unto the unity and to belief in the most high, the glorious, and that, when the whole world lay in the lap of materialism and atheism and the various idolatries.

He summoned the heathen to abandon their idols and repudiate their cults, and the 'comparers' (*al-mushabbihūn*), immersed in confusion between the holy Divine essence and the things of the material body, to purge themselves of their *tashbīh*. He called on the dualists to confess the one Divine disposition of the worlds and to bring every thing in existence under Him. He urged the naturalists to look beyond the veil of nature and see the light of the mystery of being from which it had its life. He called upon the leaders of men to humble themselves to the common rank in abasement before the one sovereign power and worship the architect of heaven and earth, who holds their spirits in life in the temples of the body.

He confronted those who laid claim to an intermediary position between the high God and His worshippers with the plain truth, manifested by revelatory light, that before God the greatest of them was no more than the least of those who gave

The Mission and Message of Muḥammad 115

them credence. He demanded they come down from their pretentious 'lordly' stations to the lowest rung of service, in identity with every soul of man and in utter reliance upon the one Lord, before whom every creature is equal, save in their differing endowments of knowledge and virtue.

In his preaching he took up the cudgels against the slaves of habit and the traditionalists, calling on them to liberate themselves from their bondage and throw off the chains withholding them from action and from hope. He had a message also for the readers of sacred scriptures, whose it was to watch over the Divine laws which they contained. He rebuked those of them who stupidly stayed over the letter and reserved a special censure for those who falsified them, giving the words a meaning not intended in the revelation, in order to indulge their passions. He summoned them to a true understanding and a realisation of their inner secret, that light from their Lord might be theirs.

He turned every man to the Divine gifts he had received and called upon all, men and women, common people and their rulers alike, to know themselves and the faculty of reason and thought with which God had specially blessed their kind, their dignity therein and their freedom of will in following the mind's direction. He assured them how God had made over to them the power to understand and exploit everything within their hands on the sole condition of moderation and conformity to the just limits of the sacred law and a true virtue. For thereby God had brought within their reach the knowledge of Himself as their creator, simply by dint of mind and thought, without any intermediary—save those upon whom in special incidence the revelation came. God has entrusted to men by proofs the things they know and likewise their knowledge of the creator of all living things. The need for the chosen prophets has to do with the knowledge of the Divine attributes which He has permitted to be known, not with the belief in their existence. He has decreed that no human has power over any other human except as laid down in the sacred law and as required by justice. Otherwise, man follows his own will and option over his affairs in accordance with his natural disposition.

The Prophet called man to understand that he is both body and spirit—two different, though inter-mingling worlds, both of which he must recognise in their claims and satisfy according to the dictates of the Divine wisdom.

He called all men likewise to make ready in this life for what awaits them in the next, and showed them that sincerity before God in worship and to His servants in justice, guidance and counsel, was the best preparation for the journey any man could make.

He fulfilled his great mission alone, with neither power nor weight of status. In all this his labour, men around proved lovers of the traditional, even at the cost of losing this world and precluding the next. They are naturally averse to what is unknown and unfamiliar, even though it means the amplest living and mastery and the very acme of happiness. People all around him were their own worst foes, slaves of their passions, uncomprehending both of his message and his mission. The attitude of the common people was tied to the evil whims of the ruling few, whose minds in turn were veiled by lust of power, unheeding of the claims of a poor illiterate like Muḥammad. They saw in him nothing to entitle him to be their counsellor or to cast reproach and reprimand upon the likes of them.

Yet for all his poverty and frailty, he plied them with arguments and taxed them with evidence. He alerted them with counsel and rebuke to all that was at stake, subjecting them to a running fire of sound exhortation, as if he were some monarch in his kingdom, enjoining or forbidding with equal justice, or a wise father nurturing his sons, vigilant and watchful for their welfare, kindly withal and merciful in his authority.

There was great strength in this weakness, power in the guise of frailty. What shall we say of such knowledge in the illiterate? What sure guidance is this amid the floods of ignorance? Is it not that he is the utterance of God almighty, whose mercy and knowledge embrace all things? Here is the executive of God, His command sounding in men's ears, cleaving the veils and shattering the enveloping walls, penetrating men's hearts. It is the word of God on the lips of His chosen servant, chosen to speak for Him, the weakest, albeit, of his people, that by this election he might be an unmistakable sign, unassailable against all suspicion, being so far unprecedented in all creation.

The Mission and Message of Muḥammad

What evidence for prophethood could be greater? An illiterate arises and calls the falsifiers to the understanding of their writing and their reading. One without the learning of the schools invites the very scholars to purify their knowledge. Denied the springs of learning he yet guides the initiates. Growing up among the deluded he proceeds to straighten the crooked paths of the wise. A stranger among the simplest of peoples and close to nature, the remotest nation from sophistication about the laws of the universe and its wonderful order, he undertakes to enunciate for all the world the principles of holy law and sketches out the ways of blessedness that none might ever perish who walks therein and none find salvation out of them.

What is this preaching that leaves detractors speechless? What is this incontrovertible thing? Let me not say that this is a gracious angel, and no man. (Surah 12.31.) No, indeed. I say as God has decreed it of him: 'He is only a man, like yourselves whom God has inspired.' (Surah 41.6.) He is a prophet who attests the prophets. He does not persuade by dazzling the sight, or puzzling the senses, or taking the feelings by surprise. Rather he requires that every faculty do its proper work. He speaks especially to reason as the judge of right and wrong. With him the force of language, the power of eloquence and the validity of the evidence are the substance of the case and the sign of truth. 'Falsehood cannot come into it from within nor from behind. It is a revelation from One who is wise and glorious.' (Surah 41.42.)

Chapter 12

THE QUR'ĀN

A recurrent tradition which is undoubtedly reliable, relates that the Prophet was, as we have indicated, brought up illiterate. It is equally maintained down the years, among the nations, that he brought a scripture of which he said that it had been sent down upon him. That Book was the Qur'ān, written on pages and preserved in the hearts of those Muslims who in their care committed it to memory, down to today.

It is a Book which contains such chronicles of the nations of the past as hold a moral for present and future generations, proving the true and jettisoning the false and imaginary, and thus alerting us to the lessons they afford.

It narrates of the prophets what God wills us to know of their story and their course of life, the issues between them and their peoples and believers in their message.

It blamed the learned leaders of the various sects for the degree to which they had corrupted their beliefs and 'alloyed' their precepts, and for the exegetical alterations they had made in their Scriptures. The Qur'ān laid down for men the principles by which their interests might be rightly served. Nothing could be clearer than the benefit which comes from being guided by them and preserving them jealously. Justice rests on them and the whole social order remains secure within their authority. Contrariwise, their neglect or abandonment, or any departure even from their spirit, entails great loss. In these ways the laws of the Qur'ān are superior to all the legislation of the nations, as will be evident to any one who studies their history.

The Qur'ān, moreover, contains rules, exhortations and moral precepts that bow men's hearts and win a kindly way into men's

The Qur'ān

minds. In their wake resolutions take their forward way, in the cause of human society.

The Qur'ān was sent down at a time when, as is widely and confidently agreed, the Arabs had reached the finest point in their history. It was an age that was copious in literary eloquence and richer than any earlier time in men of noble speech and knights of the pulpit. The most precious of intellectual pursuits and achievements in which the Arabs competed was excellence in word—the power, that is, to reach the conscience and sway the will through the art of language. There is no need here to elaborate on this, for their wholehearted absorption in their prowess is well-known.

Tradition also bears sustained witness to the fact that there was insistent opposition to the Prophet. His people used every sort of means, devious and obvious, and their utmost vigour, to crush his message, and to give the lie to all he said of God. Among them were rulers whose pride of sovereignty aroused their antagonism. There were princes concerned only for their authority. Orators, poets and writers disdained to throw in their lot with him. All these intensified their attacks with a growing spite, arrogantly refusing to acknowledge him, in their tenacity for the religion of their forebears and their determination to maintain traditional beliefs. Muḥammad held on his way, discrediting their illusions, exposing their ideas and holding their idols up to scorn. He summoned them to a faith unknown and unheralded in all their time. His only argument on its behalf was to bid them outmatch even the shortest chapter of the Book, or ten chapters. They were free to rally to this task all the learned, eloquent and literary pundits, to their heart's content, in order to rival Muḥammad's deliverances and so confound his case and put him to rout.

Yet, as the narratives make very clear, despite the long period in which the challenge lasted and the stubborn hostility in their hearts, the community was completely impotent and unsuccessful. The mighty Book was vindicated as being speech *par excellence*, and its judgements superior to all others. Is not the appearance of such a book, from the lips of an illiterate man, the greatest miracle and clearest evidence that it is not of human origin? Is it not rather the light that emanates from the sun of

Divine knowledge, the heavenly wisdom coming forth from the Lord upon the illiterate Prophet?

Furthermore, the Book brought tidings of the unseen world, which terrestrial events have confirmed. For example, the verse: 'The Greeks have been defeated in a neighbouring land, but in a few years' time they will in turn be victorious.' (Surah 30.2-3), and the explicit promise: 'God has promised assuredly to those of you who believe and do good works that He will make you masters in the land, as He did those who were before you.' (Surah 24.55), which indeed came to pass. The Qur'ān is full of such examples, as any right-minded reader will discover.

Muḥammad's awareness of the hidden world of things is implicit also in his challenge to the Arabs about producing a comparable chapter and his readiness to stake his mission on it —if one keeps in mind the extent of Arab lands, the wealth of population within their wide borders, the diffusion of his message on the part of the delegations come to Mecca from every corner, and the further fact that Muḥammad himself had not circulated in those parts or made the acquaintance of their leading men. One man's knowledge is ordinarily quite inadequate to cover the potential of so great a nation as the Arab people. We must take it then that his unhesitating assertion that they would never be able to produce anything like the Qur'ān was not a merely human judgement. It would be not only very difficult but impracticable for an intelligent person to involve himself in such an undertaking and put himself under such a pledge. Any thinking person would naturally assume that the world would not lack a match for him. Thus it is God who addresses men in these words of challenge. On Muḥammad's lips, the all-knowing, the all-ware, is speaking. God's knowledge comprehends the universal incapacity to rise to what is required and meet the challenge.

It may be falsely suggested that the argument from inability to reproduce the like applies only to those who are so unable. It is an argument, allegedly, which carries the day only with an adversary who has conceded its premises. He cannot rebut the case and so has to concede the argument. But with others it could be, in fact is, otherwise. For these are under no obligation

The Qur'ān

to yield the point or admit to being silenced, having not conceded the assumptions. Such people could find a ready way to refute inimitability.

We take this to be a false position. It cannot stand before what has been already proved. There is no comparison between the actual fact of the Qur'ān's being unmatched and a hypothetical impotence. The only thing they have in common is inability to match: but there is a world of difference between them and the fashion of the impossibility alleged. The matchlessness of the Qur'ān is an actuality beyond the powers of humanity. Its eloquence remained unparalleled. We say deliberately 'the powers of humanity'. For the Qur'ān came to an Arabic-speaking prophet. Writing was well-known among the Arabs everywhere at that time, to a degree of excellence already described, and in the context of intense hostility already noted. Yet for all that the Arabs quite failed to produce from their whole mental effort anything to oppose to it. It is then irrational to think that some Persian, or Indian or Greek, could have commanded such Arabic skill to achieve what had defeated the Arabs themselves? The powers of the Arabs quite failed them, despite their having comparable origins and education to Muḥammad, and many of them special advantages of science and study. All of this is proof positive that the words of the Qur'ān are in no way the sort of thing to originate from man. No! it was a unique Divine gift to him on whose lips it came. And so its statements about their inability to equal it and its readiness to meet head on all that their skill could contrive are plain proofs of its assurance as to its identity. The speaker is undoubtedly the Lord, who knows the unseen and the visible, and no man preaching and counselling in the ordinary way. This is the conclusion of all the evidences now accumulated, of contents quite impossible to merely human intelligence to sustain for so long.

And thus, the great wonder of the Qur'ān is proved. This eternal Book untouched by change, susceptible of no alteration, demonstrates that our Prophet, Muḥammad, is God's messenger to His creation. His message is to be believed, and the whole contents of the heaven-sent Book. It is ours to follow all that it lays down as guidance and law. It is written in the Qur'ān that

Muḥammad is the seal of the prophets and this is for us *de fide*.

It remains for us to deal in a summary form with the role of the Islamic religion and its obligations and with the rapid expansion of its message, as well as the inner meaning of the Prophet's sealing all prophecy.

Chapter 13

THE ISLAMIC RELIGION, OR ISLAM

Islam is the religion of Muḥammad's mission, as readily understood by his companions and their contemporaries who heeded it. It was actively followed among them for a period without schism or deviations in interpretation or sectarian tendencies. In this chapter it is my purpose to summarise it. In so doing I will follow the Qur'ān's own instinct which is to leave to men of alert intelligence the detailed applications, relying throughout in my remarks upon the Book, the authoritative tradition or Sunnah and the guidance of the true guides.

The religion of Islam teaches the unity of God, in His essence and His acts, and His transcendance above all comparison with created beings. It has come with proof of the universe having one creator, whose known attributes of knowledge, power, will and so forth are to be traced in the effects of His handiwork. It insists that He is incomparably other than anything in His creation: the only relation between Him and them consists in that He is their originator, that they belong to Him and unto Him is their returning. 'Say: He is God alone ... God the self-subsistent: who does not beget and is not begotten, and unto whom none is equal.' (Surah 112.1-3). When the Qur'ān speaks of 'the face', 'the hands' and 'taking His seat' and similar expressions, the Arabs whom it addresses knew well their import and were in no doubt about them. Islam holds it impossible that the essence of God and His attributes should take the shape whether of body or spirit, of any being in all the worlds. But He to whom is all praise gives to those of His servants whom He wills and as He wills some knowledge or power for the deeds He has ordained for them, within His eternal and unchanging foreknowledge. Islam forbids any rational mind, however, to acknowledge such special gifts in any man without clear evidence, the premises of which are open to sense-judgement and the related axioms are at least as clear, if not more so. Among such axioms would be that it is impossible to affirm both of two opposites, or to eliminate both of them together, or that it is necessary that the whole be greater than the part. Of prophets as well as others, Islam lays down that they cannot of themselves control good and harm (Surah 13.17). The entire truth about them is that they are honoured servants. What happens at their hands is a special activity of God's permission, by special enablement, in a particular situation and for a special and wise end. That God is truly active with them in these ways is only known, as we have said, by clear proof.

A typical note of this religion is in the verse: 'God has brought you forth from the wombs of your mothers—and you knowing nothing. He gave you hearing and seeing and a heart: perhaps you may be thankful.' (Surah 16.78.) Gratitude in Arab minds means using the grace given in loyalty to the intention within it. So in this way the Qur'ān points out that God has given us senses and implanted faculties that we may employ them in all their aspects, solely as God's gift to us. For each individual person shapes his own activity whether to his credit or his discredit.

Only God, however, has the ultimate and unique authority. It is this His power which amazes and transcends all rational conception. In its presence our souls are aware of over-mastering strength and yet a succour enabling our infirmity of understanding—a power far above all that we know in the abilities at our disposal. To Him must our submission be. To Him we ever return, our only source of aid. He alone ought we to reverence: in Him alone do our souls find tranquillity. All the fears and hopes of the soul in the life to come belong with Him. There is no proper refuge save in Him alone, whether for the acceptance of our worthy deeds or the pardoning of our evils. He alone is the disposer of the day of judgement.

Thus Islam uprooted paganism and all kindred attitudes, whatever the distinctions within them of form and image, word and term—differences which do not obscure an identity in fact. And in consequence, the minds of men were purged of the corrupting fantasies inseparable from that vain creed. Their

The Islamic Religion, or Islam

souls were likewise liberated from the evil forces belonging with their delusions and found release from the divisions that raged about objects of worship. Thus the whole level of humanity was lifted: human values responded to the new sense of human dignity implicit in worshipping none but the one creator of heaven and earth, the master of all men. Men everywhere could now say with Abraham—indeed were duty bound to say: 'I turned my face to Him who created the heavens and the earth, as a true worshipper (*ḥanīf*): I am not one of those who take other gods for God and profess as the Prophet was commanded. My prayer, my devotion, my life and my death are God's, the Lord of the worlds. He has none like unto Him. So am I commanded: I am the first of the Muslims.' (Surah 6.163.)

So man came blessedly to see himself free and honourable: his will was freed from the bonds that tied him to the will of others, whether of fellow men supposedly also an offshoot of the Divine, or of rulers and masters, or again fictitious entities to which imagination attributed powers of will, such as tombs and stones, trees and stars and the like. So man's initiative was released from the captivity to mediators, intercessors, divines, initiates, and all who claimed to be masters of 'hidden' cults and pretended to authority over the relations men have with God through their works. These 'mediators' set themselves up as disposers of salvation with the power of damnation and bliss. In sum, man's spirit found freedom from the slavery of deceivers and charlatans.

Man came by the doctrine of Divine unity to serve God's purpose only. He was no longer in bondage to another. He now had the right of one free man among free men: there were no inequalities of high and low, in respect of these rights. There was no 'inferior' and 'superior'. The only distinction between men was in their deeds: the only pre-eminence lay in intelligence and breadth of knowledge. The only drawing near to God was by the path of utter purity of mind, with sincerity and integrity of deed. Men thereby could possess their possessions, saving only the obligations to the poor and needy and the claims of the public good, and unharassed by worthless people who laid claim to them, not out of any work or service they did but from sheer position or status.

Islam requires that the able-bodied should work. Each has the right to his own gains and of his own liabilities. 'Whoever has done an atom's weight of good will see it, and whoever has done an atom's weight of evil will see it too.' (Surah 99.7-8.) 'Man will have only what he has striven for.' (Surah 53.39.) Islam allows every man to satisfy his desires in respect of food and drink, dress and adornment. It forbids him only what is injurious to him or to those within his protection, or what occasions harm to others. And for this purpose it lays down general limits adequately to preserve the interests of humanity at large. It ensures each man in his independence of action and gives wide room for competition and endeavour, without let or hindrance saving only acknowledged rights.

Islam will have no truck with traditionalism, against which it campaigns relentlessly, to break its power over men's minds and eradicate its deep-seated influence. The underlying bases of *taqlīd* in the beliefs of the nations have been shattered by Islam.

In the same cause, it has alerted and aroused the powers of reason, out of long sleep. For whenever the rays of truth had penetrated, the temple custodians intervened with their jealous forebodings. 'Sleep on, the night is pitch dark, the way is rough and the goal distant, and rest is scant and there's poor provision for the road.'

Islam raised its voice against these unworthy whisperings and boldly declared that man was not created to be led by a bridle. He was endowed with intelligence to take his guidance with knowledge and to con the signs and tokens in the universe and in events. The proper role of teachers is to alert and to guide, directing men into the paths of study.

The friends of truth are those 'who listen to what is said and follow its better way.' (Surah 39.18.) as the Qur'ān has it. It characterizes them as those who weigh all that is said, irrespective of who the speakers are, in order to follow what they know to be good and reject what gives evidence of having neither validity nor use. Islam threw its weight against the religious authorities, bringing them down from the dominance whence they uttered their commands and prohibitions. It made them answerable to those they dominated, so that these could keep an

The Islamic Religion, or Islam   127

eye on them and scrutinize their claims, according to their own judgement and lights, thus reaching conclusions based on conviction, not on conjecture and delusion.

Further, Islam encouraged men to move away from their clinging attachment to the world of their fathers and their legacies, indicting as stupid and foolish the attitude that always wants to know what the precedents say. Mere priority in time, it insisted, is not one of the signs of perceptive knowledge, nor yet of superior intelligence and capacity. Ancestor and descendant compare closely no doubt in discrimination and endowment of mind. But the latter has the advantage over his forebears in that he knows events gone by and is in a position to study and exploit their consequences as the former was not. It may be that such traceable results which men of the present generation can turn to profit will also illustrate the ill-effects of things done in earlier times and the dire evils perpetrated by the men of the past. 'Say: Go through the world and see what was the fate of those who disbelieved.' (Surah 6.11.) The doors of the Divine favour are not closed to the seeker: His mercy which embraces everything will never repel the suppliant.

Islam reproves the slavish imitation of the ancestors that characterizes the leaders of the religions, with their instinct to hold timidly to tradition-sanctioned ways, saying, as they do: 'Nay! We will follow what we found our fathers doing.' (Surah 31.21) and 'We found our fathers so as a people and we will stay the same as they'. (Surah 43.22.)

So the authority of reason was liberated from all that held it bound and from every kind of *taqlīd* enslaving it, and thus restored to its proper dignity, to do its proper work in judgement and wisdom, always in humble submission to God alone and in conformity to His sacred law. Within its bounds there are no limits to its activity and no end to the researches it may pursue.

Hereby, and from all the foregoing, man entered fully into two great possessions relating to religion, which had for too long been denied him, namely independence of will and independence of thought and opinion. By these his humanity was perfected. By these he was put in the way of attaining that happiness which God had prepared for him in the gift of mind. A certain western philosopher of the recent past has said that the growth of civilisation in Europe rested on these two principles. People were not roused to action, nor minds to vigour and speculation until a large number of them came to know their right to exercise choice and to seek out facts with their own minds. Such assurance only came to them in the sixteenth century AD—a fact which the same writer traces to the influence of Islamic culture and the scholarship of Muslim peoples in that century.

Islam through its revealed scripture took away the impediment by which the leaders of the religions had precluded rational understanding of the heavenly books on the part of their possessors or adherents, in that they arrogated the exclusive right of interpretation to themselves, withholding from those who did not share their habit or go their way the opportunity of acquiring that sacred role. They enjoined, or simply allowed, the common people to read passages from their scriptures, but on condition they should not pretend to understand or take their study far into their significance. They even went to the point of foreclosing their own critical understanding of them, or almost, on the pretext that their minds were inadequate to apprehend the contents of laws and prophecies. They restricted themselves, as well as their people, to oral reading for devotion. For sounds and letters, they abandoned the wisdom sent down to them. The Qur'ān came to convict them with the words: 'Among them are illiterate folk who do not know the Book, only as mere words they do but conjecture.' (Surah 2.78.) 'Those upon whom the burden of the Torah was laid, and they did not take it up, are likened to a donkey laden with books. Wretched is the example of those who give the lie to God's revelations. God does not guide the wrongdoers.' (Surah 62.5.)

The term *al-amānī* in Surah 2.78 is to be explained as mere readings or recitals, where the reader knows simply how to read and nothing more. If they suppose themselves to take anything from it, they do so without any knowledge of what it enjoins and with no evidence for the dogma or duty in religion which they derive from it. If it were to enter the mind of any of them, from one urge or another, to expound some aspect of the scriptures' precepts or meanings, the exegesis would be quite without any real clue. He would give some haphazard rendering and say: 'This is what God says.' But 'woe to those who write the Book with their own hands and then say: This is God's—all to make a paltry gain.' (Surah 2.79.) In referring to those who did not up the trust of the Torah, given into their very hands, the Qur'ān has in mind those who only know the words and do not enter intelligently into its injunctions and laws, and so are blind to the ways they might be guided in. Thus the tokens of guidance in the revelation are lost upon them and they well deserve the parable about the donkey, to show up their real state, so short of proper human standards. A donkey carrying books but of course getting no benefit from them for his pains—only a sore back and much panting! Can you think of a more hapless state for any folk? What inversion. The descended Book and the holy law, which should be the means of bliss, become merely a misery through ignorance and folly.

By these and similar rebukes, and by its regard for comprehension and its call for careful examination by the more able persons, leading to assurance and erudition in the law and in the contents of the Qur'ān, Islam laid upon every adherent of religion the duty of taking seriously the knowledge of revelation and of God's law. It finds all men equally so bound and able, on condition of the necessary readiness—a condition readily attainable by the vast majority of believers and in no way confined to a particular class or a peculiar time.

When Islam came, mankind was divided into religious sects and except in a few cases men were strangers to truth and certainty, quarrelling and excommunicating one another and claiming that in so doing they were holding on to the rope of God. Islam repudiated all that and affirmed unmistakeably that the religion of God through all times and by the mouth of all prophets is one. God said: 'Religion with God is Islam and those to whom the Scriptures were given disagreed among themselves through jealousy, only after knowledge had been brought to them.' (Surah 3.19.) 'Abraham was not a Jew, nor a Christian, he was a *ḥanīf*, a *muslim*, a surrendered one: he was not one of those who take gods for God.' (Surah 3.67.) 'God has decreed for you the religion which He commanded Noah: it is this which We have revealed to you, as We ordained for Abraham, Moses and Jesus, that you may perform the faith and not divide into sects.

Hard for the idolaters is that to which you call them.' (Surah 42.13.) 'Say, O people of the Book, come, hear one word which will bring us into accord. We will worship none but God and not take other gods instead of Him, and that none of us will set up other lords in His place. If they refuse, say: Bear witness that we are surrendered.' (Surah 3.64.) There are many more passages too lengthy for these pages.

The Qur'ān's reproach in such gracious verses on the people of the faith who disputed and disagreed, despite the clear case and the straight course shown to them for the knowledge of the truth over which they divided, is familiar enough to any reader of the Qur'ān who rightly ponders it.

The Book states that through all ages the religion of God is to acknowledge His Lordship alone, and to surrender in worship only to Him, to obey Him in His commands and prohibitions, as being for the welfare of humanity, and the ground of human well-being in both worlds. God has set that down in the books sent upon His chosen ones, the messengers, and to the understanding of it He calls the minds of men, just as He calls their resolution to work it out. This is the essential meaning of the faith to which one returns, when the breath of discord comes. It is the sure balance in which statements can be weighed. Wrangling and stubborn contention are then eliminated from religion as far from its ways. When its wisdom is rightly esteemed and the Divine care in the benediction it brings to humanity is seen, disagreement ends: men's hearts come back to their true guidance and as brothers they follow their proper mentors, holding fast to the truth and working together for its victory.

There are, of course, types of worship and diversities of pattern in the true religions, ancient and modern, and also varieties of precepts, new and old. But these we trace to the mercy of God and His gentleness, in shape to each people and time according to His knowledge of what is best for them. The nurture of peoples may be likened to that of individuals. God's way—the way of the Lord or nourisher of the worlds—is to proceed by stages in the nurture of a man, from the time he is born, knowing nothing, to a ripe intelligence and a mature personality, capable of penetrating the veiled mysteries of

The Islamic Religion, or Islam

existence by his reason and attaining a knowledge of them. In like manner His nurture of the nations. Neither humanity as a whole, nor particular human communities, are properly seen as staying on one constant level of knowledge and receptivity, from the day of genesis to full maturity. Rather, as earlier affirmed, society as a whole, like its individuals, is in process in line with the Divine wisdom. On truth truth there is no room for divergence of mind, though thinkers may differ in their account of it in the diversified sciences which treat of human sociology, on which we do not expatiate here.

Chapter 14

RELIGIONS AND HUMAN PROGRESS: THEIR CULMINATION IN ISLAM

When religions first began, men understood their well-being, whether general or particular, only in a most rudimentary way, rather like infants lately born, who know only what comes within their senses and distinguish only with difficulty between the present and the past. Only what they can manually touch do they really cognise, and they have no inner awareness by which to 'sympathize' with family or fellow, being concerned simply with self-preservation and too pre-occupied for the implications of their relationships with others, unless it be a hand to feed them or to steady them on their feet. Religions in that sort of context could not intelligibly relate themselves to men on subtle aspects of consciousness or 'extend' them with rational proofs. On the contrary, the great grace of God is seen in their handling the peoples as children, in just the way that a parent treats his child—with the utmost simplicity and within the senses of hearing and sight. The religions took men and gave them straight commands and firm restraints, to which they required obedience to the utmost possible degree. Though the meaning and purpose were there to be known, obedience was irrespective of actual comprehension and intelligent knowledge. Religions came with astonishing and impressive miracles and laid upon men the forms of worship consonant with their condition.

During the centuries that followed peoples flourished and declined, waxed and waned. They quarrelled and agreed. The times brought sufferings and there were endless vicissitudes of prosperity and adversity, through which they were prompted to finer sensitivity and deeper self-awareness, which may not unworthily be compared to what goes on in women's hearts or belongs with growing youth. A religion came which spoke to these feelings and, tenderly confiding to these compassions, made its appeal to the gentle arts of the heart. It laid down for men sacred laws of asceticism, drawing them away from the world altogether and turning them towards the higher life. It taught men not to press even their undoubted rights and barred the doors of heaven to the rich. Similar attitudes characterizing it are well enough known. It ordained patterns of Divine worship consistent with its understanding of man and in line with its message, and had deep effect in breaking the ills and retrieving the evils of the souls that hearkened to it. But in the course of a few generations the resolve of men grew weak and weary of it. Men lapsed from its provisions and precepts as being more than they could sustain. They took to assuming that there was an inherent impracticability in its commands. Its very custodians themselves began to rival kings for their authority and to vie in wealth with the idle rich. The great mass of people declined sadly from its noble quality through 'reinterpretation' and in their vain fancies imported all kinds of false accretions.

So things went, in respect of actions and disposition. Purity was forgotten and integrity bartered. As for dogmas, these were compromised by schism and heresy. The custodians abandoned all its principles, except one they mistakenly supposed to be its strongest pillar and chief ground, namely the veto on intellectual enquiry into faith, or indeed into the details of the universe and on the pursuit of the secret things of the mind. They promulgated the principle that reason and religion had nothing in common, but that rather religion was the inveterate enemy of science. It was not simply that this view could be taken by anyone for himself: rather they strenuously imposed it as the proper thing for all. They pressed the doctrine with such force as to provoke the most shameful of all conflicts in human history, namely civil war within the household of religion for the imposition of religious decrees. And thus the very foundations were broken up and communal relationships destroyed. Concord, co-operation and peace were ousted: schism, contention and strife reigned in their place. And so men continued until the advent of Islam.

At length, human society reached a point at which man came to his full stature, helped by the moral of the earlier vicissitudes.

Islam supervened, to present its case to reason, to call on mind and intelligence for action, to take emotion and feeling into partnership for man's guidance to both earthly and heavenly blessedness. It clarified the things that provoked human discords and demonstrated that religion with God was one in all generations, that there was a single Divine purpose for their reform without and their cleansing within. Islam taught that the sole aim of outward forms of worship was to renew the inward recollection of God and that God looks not on the form but on the heart. It required the devotee to care as well for his body as for the soul, enjoining outward as well as inward integrity, both of which it made mandatory. Sincerity was made the very heart of worship and rites were only laid down in so far as they conduced to the hallowing of moral character. 'Verily prayer preserves men from foul and evil things.' (Surah 29.45.) 'Man is created restless. When evil befalls him he despairs, but touched with good fortune he becomes niggardly—though not those who pray.' (Surah 79.19-22.) The rich man who remembers to be grateful is raised by Islam to the same level as the poor man who endures patiently. Perhaps Islam even esteems him higher. Islam deals with man in its exhortations as a wise and sober counsellor would deal with a mature person summoning him to the full harnessing of his powers, both outward and inward, and affirmed this quite unequivocally to be the way of pleasing God and showing thankfulness for His grace. This world is the seedplot of the world to come. Men will not come by ultimate good save as they endeavour a present well-doing.

Islam confronts the obdurate with the words: 'Say: bring your evidence if you are speaking the truth.' (Surah 2.111 and 27.64.) It was round with controversialists and partisans, for undermining the bases of assurance and declared that separatism was a crime, parting company as it does with manifest truth. Islam was not content with mere verbal exhortation, counsel and argument, but built concord into the fabric of law and action. It allowed the Muslim to marry with the people of the Book and partake of their table and directed that in controversy they should always be high-minded.

It is a familiar fact that kinship spreads love and binds men in amity. Inter-marriage happens only where there is mutual

Religions and Human Progress

affection between the families of the parties and ties of concord —greater factors as these are than just the love of the particular husband for his wife of another faith. God said: 'One of His signs is that He has created from among yourselves wives that you may find joy in them and He planted love and kindness in your hearts'. (Surah 30.21.) Furthermore, it was made incumbent on Muslims to defend those who became their protégés (*dhimmah*) from other communities just as they did themselves. Islam laid down that the rights and duties of these were no whit less than those of Muslims, though only a small tax was levied on them from their property, in respect of this protection. After payment of this tribute (*jizyah*) all compulsion relating to religion was forbidden. The hearts of the believers were gladdened with the words: 'O believers, you are responsible for yourselves only: he who goes astray cannot harm you if you are on the right way' (Surah 5.105). Theirs was the duty to invite men to good by the better way. They had neither right nor duty to employ any kind of force to induce people into Islam. It was worthy to penetrate men's hearts by its own light. The verse quoted does not relate to well-doing as between Muslims, since it only speaks of 'guidance' (into Islam) after the injunction to good relations has been performed. The whole purpose is to direct men to the fact that the Divine institution of religion is not for separatism, but for men's guidance into every meaning of the good.

Islam removed all racial distinctions within humanity, in the common dignity of relationship with God, of participation in human-kind, in race group and particular setting, as well as the dignity of being in the way of the highest attainments prepared of God for men. This universal dignity contrasts sharply with the exclusive claims of those who pretend to privileged status denied to others and consign allegedly inferior mortals to permanent subjection, thus strangling the very spirit of the peoples, or most of them, and reducing them to walking shadows.

Such is Islam, and the forms of Divine obedience according to its Book and authentic tradition, as befits the majesty of God and His transcendant glory beyond all likeness, and in accord with the mind and sound thinking. Prayer includes kneeling and prostration, movement and stillness, petition and entreaty, praise and ascription of greatness—all of which arise from that awareness of the Divine authority which overwhelms men and claims every energy. To Him the heart is bowed in awe and the soul brings homage. In all there is nothing beyond reason's range, except an abstruse question like why the prescribed number of ritual movements or the stone-throwing on pilgrimage—about which one can readily defer to the wisdom of the all-knowing, the ever-aware, in the knowledge that there is nothing evidently futile, or meaningless or inconsistent with the principles of thought with which God has furnished the mind.

Fasting is an abstinence which serves to impress on the spirit the greatness of God's command and a means to appreciate His gifts through foregoing them and, by exercise in His lovingkindness, to know its quality in truth. 'Fasting is prescribed for you, as it was for those before you, perhaps you may truly fear Him' (Surah 2.183.)

As for the pilgrimage ceremonies, they recall to man his most elemental needs and—if only once in his lifetime—serve notice on him forcibly of the equality among all men, in that there the distinction between rich and poor, pauper and prince, is annulled. All are present in a common garb, bare-headed, without adornment, and with the single aim of worship before God, the Lord of all the worlds. By the circumambulation of the Ka'bah and the 'running' and the 'standing' and by the touching of the Stone they perpetuate the memory of Abraham, father of faith. Yet they are well aware that none of these material things, for all their sanctity, have the power to harm or profit superstitiously. Each of the various parts of Islamic worship, when men truly submit themselves to them, proclaim the Divine transcendance and His holy separation from all that man vainly associates with him.

When will anything comparable be found in the rites of other nations, where reason goes awry and there is no clear way to the pure secrets of the unity and transcendance of God?

Islam dispelled the clouds of illusion which obscured from the mind the realities of the macrocosm of this world and the microcosm of man. It affirmed that the great signs of God in the making of the world hinge on Divine laws, laid down in the

Religions and Human Progress

eternal knowledge of God and ever abiding unchanged. Yet God's part in them must never be overlooked. On the contrary, the remembrance of Him must be alive in every act of cognizance we make. In the Prophet's words: 'The sun and the moon are signs of God: they do not suffer eclipse for any one's death, nor for his birth. If you see an eclipse let it remind you of God, and wait for the re-appearance of the light.' This confirms that all earthly phenomena follow one pattern, within the age-long care of God for the laws on which He established the universe.

Islam also drew back the curtain that obscured the conditions of human well-being, whether of persons or peoples, and of the trials with which men are beset. It made the issue unmistakeably clear in both respects. The good things which God gives some to enjoy in this life and the adversities they suffer—riches and honour, power, children, or poverty, indigence, frailty and bereavement—these may perhaps result from law-abiding integrity or intransigence and crookedness in the life of the individual concerned. But more frequently God bears with evil excesses or immoral living and leaves such people with life's pleasures here, and awaits their condign punishment in the life to come. And oftentimes He tries His faithful servants, commending their submissive acceptance of His judgements. These are they who in tribulation sincerely bow before Him and say: 'We are God's and to Him do we return.' (Surah 2.156.) Thus it is not men's anger, nor their docility, nor their inward sincerity, nor yet their active wrong-doing which affect their adversities nor yet their particular blessings, except in so far as there may be some directly causal connection in the ordinary way— poverty, for example, resulting from excessive indulgence, and humiliation from cowardice and loss of authority from injustice, or like the obvious link generally obtaining between wealth and a wise disposal of affairs and public esteem from a care for public interests. Such like sequences of cause and effect are well enough known and are not our subject here.

It is not this way, however, in respect of nations. There is a spirit from which the life of nations takes its rise, illuminating their true well-being in this world here and now, before the other world is reached. It is the spirit which God has implanted in His Divine laws for the right ordering of thought and reflection, the discipline of desire and the curbing of ambition and lust. It is the spirit which bids us assess every question on its proper merits and pursue all objectives soundly, keeping faith, holding brotherly affection and co-operating in right dealing, with mutual loyalty through thick and thin. 'He who wishes his reward in this world, We will give him thereof.' (Surah 3.145.) God will never deprive a nation of His favour as long as this spirit animates them. Rather He will multiply their blessings in proportion to its strength and diminish them when it is weak. Should the spirit no longer be found in the nation, happiness also takes its leave and peace with it. God then turns its strength into decline and its wealth to poverty. Well-being then gives way to wretchedness and peace to trouble. While they slumber in neglect, they will be overpowered by others, either by tyrants or by just masters. 'If We desire to bring a nation to destruction, We first warn those of them who live in comfort. But if they go on in sin, they bring down upon themselves a righteous judgement and We utterly destroy them.' (Surah 17.16.) God has commanded righteousness, but they have perverted it to evil. In that event, wailing and weeping will bring them no help, nor will intercession avail, nor the surviving appearances of activity. Their only hope of staying the rot is to repair again to that gracious spirit and seek its renewed descent from the heaven of mercy upon their affairs, through the promptings of thought and recollection, of patience and thanksgiving. 'Truly God does not change a people's condition until inwardly they change themselves.' (Surah 13.11.) 'This was the pattern of God's relationship to those who passed away before you: you will never find the way of God to vary.' (Surah 33.62.) There is no finer word than that spoken by 'Abbās ibn 'Abd al-Muṭṭalib when he prayed for rain: 'O God, there is no distress that comes upon us without our having transgressed: and none is lifted off us save by repentance.'

The earliest of the Islamic people lived by these laws. While the Muslim spirit was exalted by these noble beliefs and worked them out in worthy actions, other peoples supposed that by their prayers they could shake the earth and rend the heavens with their lamentations, while they wallowed in their passions and persisted in extravagant ways, so that their idle hopes of intercession profited them nothing.

The Qur'ān urges instruction and right direction for the ordinary people and kindly dealing and vetoes evil-doing. It says: 'A group from each community should stay behind to be well versed in religion, so as to admonish their people when they return, so that they may take heed.' (Surah 9.122.) It commands the same in the verse: 'Be a people who invite men to goodness, who enjoin kindly dealing and forbid what is evil. These are the prosperous ones. Do not be like those who were divided and quarrelled among themselves after clear evidence had been given them. These incur sore punishment, on the day when some faces will be radiant and others sombre. To the blackened-face sinners God will say: Did you belie your faith after you believed? Then taste the punishment. For you are unbelievers. As for those whose faces are cheerful, these will abide for ever in God's mercy. Such are the signs of God, which We recite to you in truth. God desires no injustice in His worlds. Unto Him are all things in the heavens and the earth.' (Surah 3.104–109.)

After these admonitions, which bring disquiet to the transgressors and affirm the retribution of those who defy or fall short of the Divine commands, the Qur'ān sets out the happy case of those who are steady doers of good and who shun the evil, in the plainest terms: 'You are the best people, raised up for mankind; you enjoin the good and forbid the evil and you believe in God.' (Surah 3.110). The mention of these two in this verse prior to the phrase about believing, despite the fact that faith is the source from which righteous dealing derives and the stock from which the branches of goodness spring, is to highlight that moral obligation and make it paramount. Indeed, we may say that the order of the verse witnesses to the fact that goodness is that which preserves faith and its guardian angel. The Qur'ān emphasizes its repudiation of those who neglect these things and of the religionaries who disregarded them. It says: 'The unbelievers in Israel were cursed by David, Jesus and Mary, in that they rebelled and were transgressors. They did not forbid one another the evil they committed. Their deeds were verily deplorable.' (Surah 5.78–79.) Such a malediction as was uttered against them is the most intense expression of God's wrath and abhorrence.

Islam laid down for the poor a well-defined right to the property of the rich which the latter were freely to honour, in relieving the need of the destitute, healing the distress of the afflicted, emancipating the enslaved and helping 'the sons of the way'—the homeless people. It held such expenditure in the pursuit of goodness the most urgent of all its exhortations, making it oftentimes the token of faith and a sign of having been guided into 'the straight path.' By this means it neutralized the grudges of the poor and cleansed their hearts from envy at the bounty with which God had blessed the well-to-do and thus conduced to a mutual charity of heart between the two. Compassion in the wealthy for the lot of the wretched brings tranquillity to all. Where is there a more salutary cure for the ills of society? 'That is God's grace which He bestows on whomsoever He wills: For God is the Lord of great magnanimity.' (Surah 57.21.)

Islam also barred the way to two evils and cut off two copious sources of wickedness in outlawing wine and gambling and usury —which it did absolutely and without compromise.

From all the foregoing, it is clear that Islam has not omitted to treat of any one of the basic virtues. There is no important aspect of good conduct in which it has not brought a new lease of life—nothing essential to the social fabric it has failed to enjoin. As we have shown, it brings together for mature man, freedom of thought, intellectual independence of action, and thus integrity of character, enhancement of capacity and a general quickening of intention and achievement. Whoever reads the Qur'ān rightly will find new impulse and initiative and unfailing treasure.

When one has sound training, does one need a mentor; or a guardian when one's mind is fully ripe? Hardly! for the true has been distinguished from the false and all that remains is to follow the guidance and from the hands of mercy take the way that brings one to happiness here and hereafter.

For this reason, Muḥammad's prophethood brought prophecy itself to an end. His message terminated the work of messengers, as the Book affirms and the authentic tradition corroborates.

The fact is evidenced by the collapse of all pretensions to prophethood since Muḥammad, as well as by the world's contentment with the truth that has come to it from him. The world knows that there is no acceptability now in claims made by pretenders after mission with laws and revelation from God. It acknowledges the heavenly word which says: 'Muḥammad is not the father of any man among you. He is the messenger of God and the seal of the prophets. God truly knows all things.' (Surah 33.40.)

Chapter 15

THE EXPANSION OF ISLAM: ITS UNPARALLELED SPEED

The need of the nations for reformation was one which they all shared, so God made the mission-message of the final Prophet universal. Even so the intelligent observer of human events is left in utter amazement at the way in which Islam gathered the whole of the Arab nation from end to end into its allegiance in less than thirty years, and then embraced other nations from the western ocean to the borders of China in less than one century. No other religion has a comparable story and for that very reason many have missed the real explanation. But the fair-minded understood and left no cause for idle wonderment.

Like other religions, Islam began with its message. But it encountered a quite unprecedented enmity on the part of those who in their perversity oppressed the truth. No prophet had such antagonism or faced such humiliation as Muḥammad—trials which he would never have survived without God's protection. Those who responded to his message were brow-beaten, denied food and ejected from their homes. Much blood was shed. When blood seals faith it is as if springs of high resolves are set flowing from the hard rocks of patient endurance. At the sight of it, God strengthened the righteous and struck misgiving into the obdurate. It might be compared to a surgeon's blood-letting by which the body is rid of its corruption. For at the sight of it some of the dubious folk were melted in heart and their evil purged: 'That God may separate the bad from the good and gathering the bad together cast them as one into hell. Truly these are the lost.' (Surah 8.37.)

The different religious sects inhabiting the Arabian peninsula and neighbouring areas joined forces against Islam to root it out and strangle its message. It was a case of the strong against

The Expansion of Islam

the weak, the wealthy against the poor. Islam in its steadfast self-defence had nothing to rely on save its inherent truth, pitted against error and the light of its guidance in the darkness of falsehood, to bring it to victory. Thus it gathered strength. Tribes in the Arabian peninsula of other religious allegiance were very active in propagating their creeds and had rulers, power and authority all on their side, and stooping to cunning devices to further their ends. Nevertheless they achieved little and their forceful methods proved barren.

Islam cemented the desert peoples of Arabia into a unity hitherto unknown. There was nothing like it in their history. The Prophet extended his mission by God's command, to neighbouring territories, to the emperors of Persia and of Greece. But they scorned him, proscribed his message and evil-intreated both him and his people. They intimidated the caravans and waylaid the merchandise, to which Muḥammad replied with raids, sending deputations to their countries, as did the Caliphs his companions after his death, demanding safe passage and the acceptance of his message. The Muslims, despite their weakness and poverty, took the truth in their hands and went forth in its defence. They waged war against the superior enemy and overcame them, for all their vast numbers, strength and advanced equipment. When the distresses of war were spent and sovereignty passed to the victor, Islam treated the vanquished with kindly gentleness, allowed them to maintain their religions and their rites in security and peace. They gave them protection and safeguarded their possessions, as they did their own people and their property, levying for this service a slight tax on their incomes according to stipulated rates.

When non-Muslim powers conquered a kingdom they used to follow the army of conquest with an army of preachers of their faith, who took up quarters in the houses and occupied their councils, in order to impose the conqueror's religion. Their argument was force and their evidence conquest. It was not so with Muslim victors: such things were quite unknown in all their history. There were no preachers with the official and special duty to undertake propaganda and give their whole energies to urging their creed on non-Muslims. Instead the Muslims contented themselves with mixing among other peoples

The Theology of Unity

and treating them kindly. The entire world witnessed that Islam counted the proper treatment of conquered peoples a meritorious and virtuous thing, whereas Europeans regard such behaviour as weak and despicable.

Islam lightened the heavy burden of tribute payment and restored plundered property to its owners and dispossessed those who had extorted their unlawful gains. It gave equality before the law to Muslim and non-Muslim.

Subsequently it became a regulation that no one be accepted into Islam except before a judge of the sacred law who required from the new Muslim a declaration that he had become a Muslim without duress and without personal self-interest. Under some of the Umayyad Caliphs it even happened that the district administrators looked with strong disfavour on Islamizing, because of the resultant decrease in the tax yield of the *jizyah*, or tribute. Such officials were undoubtedly a deterrent to the spread of the faith and for that reason 'Umar ibn 'Abd al-'Azīz ordered that they should be reprimanded.

The Muslim Caliphs and rulers in all periods recognized the skills of various kinds which some of the people of the Book, and others too, possessed. They brought them into their service and gave them the highest positions even to the point of putting them in command of the armies in Spain.

Such was the fame of Islamic lands for freedom of religion that Jews from Europe migrated, as for example to Andalusia, and elsewhere, seeking sanctuary for their religion.

So much for the benign policy of Muslims towards those whom their swords guarded. Their only concern was to bring to these peoples the Book of God and His holy law, which they offered them in full freedom either to accept or refuse. They did not preach among them and used no forcible methods to induce faith. Nor was the tribute tax in any way onerous. What then was it which drew the adherents of the various faiths into Islam and convinced them that in Islam, rather than in their ancestral beliefs, the truth lay, so that they espoused it en masse and even outdid the Arabs themselves in its zealous service?

The triumph of Islam over the various pagan rites of the Arabian peninsula, its victory over the vicious pagan practices and evil ways, and its success in leading the inhabitants to

The Expansion of Islam

uprightness and excellence of character, made the readers of earlier scriptures realize that here was the fulfilment of God's promise to Abraham or Ismāʻīl. Herein was the answer to the prayer of the former, the friend of God: 'O our Lord, send among them a messenger from their own ranks.' (Surah 2.129.) This is the religion which the prophets proclaimed to their peoples after them. The just folk among them could no longer hold out in obstinate resistance to it, but gratefully embraced it and patiently abandoned their patrimony.

These conversions occasioned much heart-searching among those who held by their traditions and aroused them to look into Islam, where they met with kindliness and compassion, with goodness and grace, not a creed which scared away reason. For reason is the pioneer of authentic belief. Nor is it in any way onerous for human nature, which is the true criterion of what best serves and befits human needs. They saw that Islam lifts the souls of men by an awareness of the Divine to a point where men almost transcend the lower world and become a part of the heavenly kingdom. Islam invites men to the daily renewal of that awareness of God through the five times of prayer, yet for all that it does not impede the delight of pleasurable things. It does not impose disciplines and acts of asceticism that would be a burden upon natural human proclivities. It considers that the body should have its rights consistently with pure conscience and proper intention and takes such an attitude to be pleasing to God and meritorious. If any man is carried away by passion and succumbs, there is Divine forgiveness for him when he duly repents and turns back.

Readers of the Qur'ān were much impressed with the simplicity of this religion and the way of life of its true and pure followers had great appeal. They realized the difference between the incomprehensible creeds and one whose essentials could be taken in at a glance. They almost stampeded into it to be free of the heavy, oppressive thing they endured.

Now the nations had what they were looking for—a religion with a mind to think. Now they had a faith which gave justice its due place. The main factor which deterred a massive and spontaneous accession to Islam to enjoy these things long-desired lay in the system of class privilege under which the nations laboured. By this some classes lorded it over others, without right. Rulers recked nothing of the interests of the common people if the desires of the higher classes conflicted with them. Here was a religion which regulated human rights and gave equal respect to persons of all classes, their beliefs, their dignity and their property. It gave, for example, to a poor non-Muslim woman the perfect right to refuse to sell her small dwelling, at any price, to some great amir, ruling absolutely over a large territory, who wanted it, not for private purposes, but in order to enlarge a mosque. When, in this particular case, he doubled the price and took forcible steps to acquire it and she raised a complaint to the Caliph, he issued an order to ensure her possession and reproached the amir for his action. Islamic justice permitted a Jew to take up a case before the judge against no less a person than 'Alī ibn Abī Ṭālib, who was made to stand with the plaintiff in the court-process until judgement was given.

The foregoing makes clear how the message and relationships Islam brought endeared even its enemies to it, and so revolutionized their outlook as to make them its allies and protégés.

Muslims were consistently motivated by the spirit of Islam through all periods. They were naturally disposed to friendship with their non-Muslim neighbours. Nor did they harbour enmity in their hearts towards those who differed from them, as long as the latter refrained from coercing them. It was from such hostile neighbours that the Muslims learned hatred and then only in a transient way. Once the causes of the animosity were terminated their hearts reverted readily to the earlier benevolence and easy relationships. Thus despite the negligence of their faith on the part of Muslims and their disloyalties and despite the efforts of many, intelligently or otherwise, to undermine it, Islam continued to expand, especially in China and Africa. The spectacle of numerous people of other communities coming into Islam was an uninterrupted phenomenon—and adopting doctrines with open eyes, with no sword behind them and no inciter before them. They were prompted only by what they had seen of Islam's precepts with as yet little intellectual scrutiny of its laws.

The Expansion of Islam

Thus the speed of Islam's expansion and the welcome men of every community gave to its doctrine derived from the ease with which it could be understood, the simplicity of its principles and the justice of its laws. In a word, human nature in its need for a religion, demands one that is nearest to the interests of human nature and most akin to their hearts' emotions, one which offers security in both worlds. A religion meeting these criteria will find an effective way into the hearts and minds of men, without recourse to propagators consuming large sums and much time in order to multiply means and devise stratagems to way-lay people into accepting it.

This was the case with Islam in its original simplicity and the pristine purity in which God shaped it, and which it has continued in large measure to maintain in many parts of the world to this day.

Those who do not understand, or have no will to understand, all this say that Islam only expanded at this pace by dint of the sword. The Muslims conquered the territories of men with the Qur'ān in one hand and the sword in the other. They offered the Qur'ān to the defeated and if it was not accepted their life was forfeit. Forsooth! this is a great slander. Our earlier account of the way Muslims handled accessions to their authority is steadily authenticated by the chronicles and there can in general be no doubt whatever about it, even if there are disparities of detail. The Muslims only used the sword in self-defence and in retaliation against aggression. Subsequently opening up of those territories to conquest was a necessity of statecraft. Otherwise good neighbourliness and immunity was the principle of Muslim relationships and a way whereby Islam came to be known for what it was. The need for better intellectual and practical standards was a powerful factor leading men to adopt it.

Were the sword to propagate religion, the pursuit of such violent methods of compulsion would constitute a threat to every nation not accepting it—a mortal threat of annihilation from the face of the earth. This would need overwhelmingly large armies and the utmost expenditure of force. Such things had been initiated three whole centuries before the rise of Islam and continued for seven centuries more after Islam appeared. But those ten entire centuries of sword-propagation did not achieve what Islam accomplished in respect of accession of believers in less than one century. Add to that vain sword in those centuries, and following it at every step, the preachers saying what they will behind the security of the sword, and, withal, a spate of zeal and eloquence, and money to turn the hearts of the wavering—and all in vain! Surely all that is sign enough for those who are open to conviction.

How splendid is the wisdom of God in the pattern of Islam. It was a river of life welling up in the desert of Arabia, the remotest part of God's earth from civilization. It flowed out to cover and to embrace in one the territories it renewed, bringing to them a vitality, both popular and communal, so far-reaching that it included kingdoms whose people boasted of even heaven's glories and whose cultural achievements had no earthly equals. The reverberations of Islam gently loosened the stony hardness of men's spirits, releasing the vital secrets that lay within them. To the charge that Islam was not innocent of militant conquest provocatively, we reply that there is a Divine imperative by which the struggle in the created world between right and wrong, good and evil, is unrelenting, until God gives the verdict. If God brings spring upon the barren land to renew its dead wastes, and with moisture slakes its thirst so that fertility returns, will that be of less worth because in the course of it He removes some obstacles in His path and even a fine built house has to be destroyed?

The light of Islam shone in the lands where its devotees went, and the only factor at work in their relation with the local people was the Word of God heard and apprehended. At times the Muslims were pre-occupied with their own affairs and fell away from the right path. Then Islam halted like a commander whose allies have disappointed him and is about to give ground. 'God brings about what He intends.' (Surah 65.3.) The Islamic lands were invaded by the Tartar peoples, led by Jenghiz Khan, pagans who despoiled the Muslims and were bent on total conquest, plunder and rapine. But it was not long before their successors adopted Islam as their religion and propagated it among their kin with the same consequences as elsewhere. They came to conquer the Muslims and they stayed to do them good.

The Expansion of Islam 149

The west made a sustained attack against the east, involving all the kings and peoples, and continuing more than two hundred years, during which time the west engendered a quite unprecedented zeal and fervour for religion. With military forces and preparations to the utmost of their capacity, they advanced towards the Muslim hearth-lands, fired by religious devotion. They overran many countries of Islamic allegiance. Yet in the end these violent wars closed with their evacuation.

Why did they come and why did they return? The religious leaders of the west successfully aroused their peoples to make havoc of the eastern world and to seize the sovereignty over those nations on what they believed to be their prescriptive right to tyrannize over masses of men. They came in great numbers of all sorts of men, estimated in millions, many settling in Muslim territory as residents. There were periods of truce in which the angry fires abated and quieter tempers prevailed, when there was even time to take a look at the surrounding culture, pick up something from the medley of ideas and react to what was to be seen and heard. It became clear that the exaggerations of their idle dreams which had shaped into such grievous efforts had no vestage of truth. And, furthermore, they found freedom in a religion where knowledge, law and art could be possessed with entire certitude. They discovered that liberty of thought and breadth of knowledge were means to faith and not its foes. By God's will they acquired some experience of refined culture and went off to their own territories thrilled with what they had gained from their wars—not to mention the great gains the travellers gathered in the lands of Andalusia by intercourse with its learned and polished society, whence they returned to their own peoples to taste the sweet fruits they had reaped. From that time on, there began to be much more traffic in ideas. In the west the desire for knowledge intensified and concern grew to break the entail of obscurantism. A strong resolve was generated to curb the authority of religious leaders and keep them from exceeding the proper precepts of religion and corrupting its valid meanings. It was not long after that a party made its appearance in the west calling for reform and a return to the simplicities of the faith—a reformation which included elements by no means unlike Islam. Indeed, some of the reforming groups brought their doctrines to a point closely in line with the dogma of Islam, with the exception of belief in the prophetic mission of Muḥammad. Their religion was in all but name the religion of Muḥammad; it differed only in the shape of worship, not in meaning or anything else.

Then it was that the nations of Europe began to throw off their bondage and reform their condition, re-ordering the affairs of their life in a manner akin to the message of Islam, though oblivious of who their real guide and leader was. So were enunciated the fundamental principles of modern civilization in which subsequent generations as compared with the peoples of earlier days have found their pride and glory.

All this was like a copious dew falling on the welcoming earth, which stirs and brings forth a glad growth of every kind. Those who had come for strife, stayed to benefit and returned to benefit others in turn. Their rulers thought that in stirring up their peoples they would find an outlet for their rancour and secure their own power. Instead they were shown up for what they were and their authority foundered. What we have shown about the nature of Islam, well enough known to every thoughtful student, is acknowledged by many scholars in western countries and they know its validity and confess that Islam has been the greatest of their mentors in attaining their present position. 'God's is the final issue of all things.' (Surah 22.41.)

Chapter 16

A READY OBJECTION

It is said by some that if Islam truly came to call diverse peoples into one common unity and if the Qur'ān says: 'You have nothing to do with those who divide over religion and make parties,' (Surah 6.159) how does it come about that the Islamic community has been sundered into sectarian movements and broken up into groups and schools?

If Islam is a faith that unifies, why this numerous diversity among Muslims? If Islam turns the believer in trust towards Him who created the heavens and the earth, why do multitudes of Muslims turn their faces to powerless things that can neither avail nor harm, and apart from God are helpless either way, even to the point of thinking such practice part of *Tauḥīd* itself?

If it was the first religion to address the rational mind, summoning it to look into the whole material universe, giving it free rein to range at will through all its secrets, saving only therein the maintenance of the faith, how is it that Muslims are content with so little and many indeed have closed and barred the door of knowledge altogether, supposing thereby that God is pleased with ignorance and a neglect of study of His marvellous handiwork?

How does it happen that the very apostles of love have become in these days a people who nose around for it in vain? They who were once exemplary in energy and action are now the very picture of sloth and idleness?

What are all these accretions to their religion, when all the time Muslims have the very Book of God as a balance in which to weigh and discriminate all their conjectures and yet its very injunctions they abandon and forsake?

If Islam really is so solicitous for the minds and hearts of men, why today in the opinion of so many is it somehow beyond the reach of those who would grasp it?

If Islam welcomes and invites enquiry into its contents, why is the Qur'ān not read except by chanting and even the majority of the educated men of religion only know it very approximately?

If Islam granted to reason and will the honour of independence, how is it that it has bound them with such chains? If it has established the principles of justice, why are the greater part of its rulers such models of tyranny? If religion eagerly anticipates the liberation of slaves, why have Muslims spent centuries enslaving the free?

If Islam regards loyalty to covenants, honesty and fulfilment of pledges, as being its very pillars, how does it come about that deception, falsehood, perfidy and calumny are so current among Muslims?

If Islam forbids fraud and treachery and warns imposters that they have neither part nor lot in it, how is it that Muslims practise deception against God, the sacred law and the true and loyal believers? If it prohibits all abomination, whether evident or hidden, what is it we see among them, both secret and open, both physical and spiritual?

If Islam teaches that religion consists in sincerity before God, His apostle and fellow-believers in both immediate and general relationships, if 'man is the loser, save those who believe, do good works and enjoin upon each other justice and patience (Surah 103.1–3) and yet, not enjoining kindliness or forbidding evil, they go altogether to the bad and their honest folk call and get no response, and if this which they quite fail to fulfill is in fact their most bounden duty, why is it that they thus so totally fail to counsel each other and lay upon each other squarely what the Divine will requires? Why do they not hold to it with fortitude and speak truth about right and wrong? Why do they in fact take each their own way, letting things go as they will in rabid individualism, ignoring each other's affairs as if they were totally unrelated the one to the other, having nothing in common? Why do sons murder fathers and daughters prove refractory towards their mothers? Where are the bowels of mercy? of

A Ready Objection

compassion for a neighbour? Where is the just dealing the rich owe to the poor with their possessions? Rather the rich plunder even what remains in the hands of the wretched.

A glimmer of Islam, it is said, illuminated the west but its full light is in the east. Yet precisely there its own people lie in the deepest gloom and cannot see. Does this seem intelligible? Is there any parallel in the annals of men? Does it not appear that the very Muslims who have known something of science are precisely those who, for the most part, instinctively regard Islam's doctrines as superstitious and its principles and precepts as a farce? They find pleasure in ape-ing the free-thinking people who scoff and jeer and think themselves forward-looking. Do you not see Muslims whose only business with the scriptures is to finger their pages, while they preen themselves on being memorizers of their precepts and expert in their laws? How far they are from the rational study of the Qur'ān which they despise and regard as worthless to religion and the world! Many of them simply pride themselves on ignorance, as if thereby they had evaded prohibited things and achieved some distinction. Those Muslims who stand on the threshold of science see their faith as a kind of old garment in which it is embarrassing to appear among men, while those who deceive themselves that they have some pretension to be religious and orthodox believers in its doctrines regard reason as a devil and science as supposition. Can we not, in the light of all this, call God, His angels and all men to witness that science and reason have no accord with this religion?

THE ANSWER

It may well be that the foregoing has not exaggerated the plight of Muslims today, indeed, these several generations past. But is the objection the whole story? Parallels could be found in the descriptions of Islam in their day given by Al-Ghazālī, Ibn al-Ḥājj and other writers on religion, filling whole volumes, both about the general population and the intelligentsia. But the reading of the Qur'ān suffices of itself to vindicate what I have said about the essential nature of Islamic religion, provided it is read with care to understand its real import, interpreted according to the understanding of those among whom it was sent down and to the way they put it into practice. To admit the validity of what I have said of its fine effects, it suffices to read the pages of history as indited by those who truly knew Islam and the objective writers in other nations. Such Islam was—and is. We have earlier said that religion is guidance and reason. Whoever uses it well and takes its directives will gain the blessedness God has promised to those who follow it. As a medicine for human society its success when truly tried is so manifest that not even the blind and the deaf can deny or gainsay it. All that the objection just elaborated leads to is this: a physician treated a sick man with medicine and he recovered: then the doctor himself succumbed to the disease he had been treating. In dire straits from pain and with the medicine by him in the house, he has yet no will to use it. Many of those who come to visit him or seek his ministrations or even gloat over his illness could take up the medicine and be cured, while he himself despairs of life and waits either for death or some miraculous healing.

We have now set forth the religion of Islam and its true character. As for those Muslims who by their conduct have become an argument against it, these must be dealt with not here, but in another book, if God wills.

Chapter 17

ACCEPTING THE TRUTH OF MUḤAMMAD'S MESSAGE

After the confirmation, by the foregoing decisive evidences of the prophethood of Muḥammad and his message from God most high, there can be no doubt that his witness ought to be received as true and his message accepted with faith. By his message, or what he brought, we mean the affirmations of the Qur'ān and whatever is consistently and authentically reported in the tradition, under the proper conditions, namely what is related by a community of persons whom it is impossible should be in collusion to deceive, of things generally within sense experience. It is also necessary to believe what is related about conditions after death and about resurrection and blessedness in the Garden and retribution in the Fire, and of the reckoning of good and evil done in life, and other familiar themes.

As far as doctrine is concerned, it is obligatory to limit ourselves to what has been formally given in the predication (in the Qur'ān and tradition). It is not permissible to add conjectures to what is absolute. A condition of true dogma is that it contains no compromise of transcendence (*tanzīh*). and the exaltedness of God above all likeness to His creatures. If anything comes in the dogma which seems to involve such compromise, that which apparently does so must be repudiated as far as that sense is concerned. We must either fall back upon God, deferring to His knowledge of the real meaning and holding that the apparent sense is not intended, or we must interpret it by what is acceptable in the context.

As for items which have only one narrator, he to whom the tradition has come, who has satisfied himself of the truth of what it contains, is obliged to believe it. But he to whom it has not come, or receiving it had misgivings about its validity, he cannot be blamed as an unbeliever if he withholds acceptance of it, since it is not verified by sustained narration. The core of this whole matter is this: he who denies something he knows the Prophet said or affirmed impugns the truth of his message and characterizes it as lies. Of the same order is neglecting to recognize what is given by unbroken tradition. For unbroken tradition is obligatorily part of the faith. This covers the contents of the Qur'ān and a few only of the traditions, or Sunnah, dealing with practical things.

He who believes in the mighty Book and in its laws relating to actions, who finds it difficult to understand the predications about the unseen world in their apparent meaning, but who makes venture at rational exegesis, relying on proven facts, while holding firmly to an actual faith in life after death and reward or retribution for works and beliefs, provided always that his exegesis diminished nothing of the significance of promise or warning or of the structure of the sacred law and its injunctions—this man is considered a true believer, though it would be unsound for him to regard his exegesis as a pattern for all. The Divine laws were given, not for the pleasing exercise of intellectual ingenuity among the élite, but for attainment by the generality of men. In short, faith is the certainty in believing in God, His apostles and the Last Day, with no other stipulation saving a reverence for the words and message of the apostles.

Two questions remain, having a place of importance in theology, though not more so than the other issues which it has been well for us to discuss in the foregoing. The first has to do with the beatific vision of God most high in the life to come; the second relates to the miracles or supernatural deeds wrought by the saints and men of truth other than the prophets.

As concerns the vision of God, there has been intense controversy which has terminated, among those who hold the doctrine of transcendence, in an agreement which leaves no room for further debate. Those 'transcendental' theologians who affirm that there is a vision of God are of one mind that the vision is not to be thought of in terms of ordinary visual perception such as we know in normal life. It is, on the contrary, a vision which has no like and no definition, and belongs only with a special sight which God will bestow upon the dwellers in

Accepting the Truth of Muḥammad's Message 157

the heavenly world or else with a changed form of our earthly sight. In either case it is impossible to know what the vision will be, though we believe that it will be, since the word of it is sound. Those who deny its possibility are still left with the fact that there is a disclosure which must be taken as equal to seeing and it is all the same whether it be by some quite new visual perception or by another sense altogether. In either case we come back to what the sceptics' opponents say. People who love contention are an affliction to Islam: but God is above all their suppositions.

As for the second question, Abū Isḥāq al-Isfirā'īnī, one of the most notable disciples of Al-Ash'arī, denied that such miracles could occur. So also did the Mu'tazilites, except Abū-l-Ḥusain al-Baṣrī and most of the Ash'arites, who upheld the possibility. The latter relied for their conviction on the story in the Qur'ān about the man, deeply versed in the scriptures, which comes in the account of the Queen of Sheba—the man, that is, who brought her throne (to Solomon) within the twinkling of an eye (Surah 27.41). And there is the story of Mary and how provision came to her, and the story of the masters of the cave.

But the other school of thought protests that this only causes confusion with the prophetic miracles. They have their own interpretation of the verses in the Qur'ān. It is, however, not true to say that there is confusion with the prophetic miracles, for the reason that the latter only occur in association with the prophetic message and the preaching from God, which must necessarily be accompanied by distinctive events to mark it off from other things.

Those who accept the feasibility of these miracles have a non-proven case, when they cite the Qur'ān. What is related about Mary and Āṣif (the transporter of the Queen of Sheba's throne) may well be a peculiar or special favour of God, happening in the times of the prophets. And we have quite insufficient knowledge of what such events involved in prophetic situations and how they belong with God's purposes.

The story of the cave (Surah 18) is divinely reckoned as one of the signs of the created order. God has brought it to our notice to give us a lively sense of what His power is in its manifestation. It does not help, therefore, in resolving the broad question of saint-miracles, which is to be related to general investigation of the powers of the human soul, their bearing on the whole world of existence, their connection with good works and with the degrees of perfection open by God's grace to the souls of men. All this is a deep, psychological study which belongs elsewhere.

As for our holding a conviction in general as to the feasibility of Divine power effectuating supernatural events through men other than prophets, I do not imagine it would give rise to much controversy among intelligent thinking people. What, however, is imperative to keep in mind is that true Muslims of all shades and sects are unanimous that there is no obligation to believe in any such miracles on the part of a 'saint' since the rise of Islam. It is permissible for every Muslim, by communal consensus, to deny the occurrence of any 'miracle' whatever from any saint, whoever he be. Such denial in no way contravenes anything in the fundamentals of Islam and in no way deviates from authentic tradition. It is in no sense an aberration from 'the straight path'. The only exception would be something attested in the tradition about the companions of the Prophet.

How far this inclusive and unanimous principle is from the ill-considered proneness of contemporary Muslims—great numbers of them—to suppose that 'miracles' and supernatural phenomena happen freely, made to order so to speak, with 'saints' in mutual rivalry in the trade and the 'pure' in whom the events have their axis taking glory against each other—all of which has nothing whatever to do with God or religion, or with the saints, or with any rational intelligence.

CONCLUSION

'God has promised those who believe and do good works to give them an empire in the earth as He gave their ancestors dominion before them, in order to strengthen the religion He chose for them and to transform their fears thereafter into security. Let them worship Me and serve no other gods beside Me. Any who after this deny the faith they are indeed evil-doers.' (Surah 24.55.)

'When we heard His guidance we believed in Him. He who believes in his Lord will never fear loss or adversity. Some of us are Muslims and some are wrongdoers. Those who embrace Islam follow the true path, but those who go astray become the fuel of hell. Had they gone in the right way, We would have sent them copious rain and thereby have put them to the test. He who gives no heed to the warning of his Lord, will be overtaken by a condign retribution. Mosques are God's: do not invoke therein any god but He. When His servant (Muḥammad) rose up to call upon Him, they congregated round him. Say: I pray to my Lord and ascribe deity to none but He. Say: I have no control over what happens to you, either of evil or of good. Say: None can ever protect from God and I will never find any refuge save in Him. My sole responsibility is with God's message and the revelation with which He sent me. Whoever rebels against God and His messenger will be for ever in the fire of Jahannam. When they see the reality they had been warned of then they will know who had the weaker source of succour and the less numerous protector. Say: I cannot tell whether the retribution is near or whether my Lord has put it off for many days. He only holds the unknown in knowledge and its secrets He does not divulge to any, except to a chosen apostle. He causes a guardian to go before His messengers and come behind them to know whether they have delivered the message of their Lord. He is about all their way and takes count of every thing.' (Surah 72.13–28.)

God has spoken truth. He is most great. The gracious apostle has brought that truth. The accursed Devil is in full flight. Most meet it is to give thanks unto God, Lord of the worlds, the merciful Lord of mercy.

Index

'Abbāsid dynasty, 35
'Abd al-Azīz, 'Umar ibn, 34
'Abdallāh ibn Saba, 32-3
'Abd-al-Muṭṭalib (grandfather of Muḥammad), 111, 113
Abraham, 99-100, 125; Islam's view of, 129
Abū Bakr al Bāqillānī, 36
Abū Ishāq al-Isfarā 'īnī, 157
Abū-l- Hasan al- Ash'arī, 36, 37, 157
Abū-l-Ma'ālī al Juwaynī, 36, 64
Abū Tālib (uncle of Muḥammad), 111
'acquisition' of faith, 64, 65, 73
Africa, Islam's expansion into, 33, 146
after-life
  concepts and secrets of the, 71, 74-5, 81-3; Muḥammad's preparation of man for the, 116
Al-'Aḍad, 38
Al-Baiḍāwī, 38
Al-Ghazālī, 37, 38, 153
'Alī (Caliph), 32-3
Al-Isfirā'inī, 36
Al-Manṣūr, 35
Al-Rāzī, 37
Al-Zahrā, 34
Arab nation
  evil practices in, 111; intellectual achievements in, 119; Muḥammad and the, 119-21; Islam as unifying force in, 143
Aristotle, 38, 105
asceticism, Islam's attitude to, 145
Ash'arites' views on miracles, 157
atheism, dissemination of, 35

beauty, man's sense of, 67-8
Being, the necessary, 45—52: see also existence; God
Byzantium, conditions and strife in, 109-10

Caliphate and Islamic teaching, 32-5
cause, concepts of, 42-3
cave, the story of the (miracle), 157-8
China, Islam's expansion into, 146
choice
  freedom of, 50-1; deeds of, 68

composite and non-composite, 45-6
contingent, the
  principles of, 40-3; real existence and, 43-4; and the necessary Being, 46; and knowledge, 47-8
conversions to Islamic faith, 144-5
credulity, the Qur'ān's teaching on, 39

deeds, good and evil, 31, 62-75; the prophets' guidance on, 102
dependence, 42
Divine law, 76 ff.
Divine secrets, the evil of trying to penetrate, 65, 74-5
divisions and disagreements, the Qur'ān's condemnation of, 129-30
dress and ornament, Islam and man's desire for, 126

Egyptians' adoption of Islam, 33
equality of all classes, Islam's policy of, 146
eternity, 45; man's incomprehension of, 55
existence, principles of, 42-4; the necessarily existing, 45-52
expansion of Islam, 33, 142-50

faith, man's 'acquisition' of, 64, 65, 73
false cults and mediators, freeing of man from, 125
food and drink, Islam and man's desire for, 126
freedom of man
  delusion of the, 63; Islam as man's liberator, 125

gains and liabilities, man's right to his, 126
gambling, Islam's view of evil of, 140
God
  concepts of attributes of, 31, 34, 39, 45-56; acts and wisdom of, 57-61; man's delusions about omnipotence of, 63 ff.; unity as special attribute of, 51-2, 123-5;

The Theology of Unity

God (contd)
  allness of, 124; His mercy towards diversities in religious patterns, 130; controversies over the vision of, 156–7
gregariousness as a characteristic of man, 85–6, 91

happiness and misery, sources of, 72–4, 140
Hasan al-Basrī, 34
healing powers of the prophets, 97
help in comprehension of the Divine mysteries, man's need of, 74–5
heresies and schisms, 34–9: see also divisions
hermits, 85

idolatry, 111
imagination, function of, 72–3
impossible, principle of the, 40
independence of will, thought and opinion, 127, 140
intellect
  rôle of, in Islamic thought, 33; eviction of, by false ideas, 39
intelligence
  degrees of, 95; Islam and the endowment of, 126

Jenghiz Khan, invasions of, 148
Jesus Christ, 99–100, 129

Kalām (scholastic theology), 30
Khadījah (wife of Muḥammad), 113
Khawārij (religious sect), 33
knowledge
  the categories of, 41–4; and the necessary Being, 47–9; man's lack of, as bar to religious conviction, 95

language, shortcomings of, 56, 61
liberation of man, Islam and the, 140
life, concepts of, 46–7
logic, distinction of, from scholastic theology, 30
love
  rôle of, in man's spiritual life, 86–9 *passim*; the prophets and revelation of secrets of, 102

magnanimity towards conquered peoples, Islam's policy of, 143–4
man, peculiar characteristics and nature of, 65, 85–92
Mecca
  as Muḥammad's birthplace, 111; as centre of Islam, 120
memory, function of, 72–3
messengers, God's: *see* prophets
miracles, 156–8
monotheism and polytheism, 76–7; *see also* unity
Moses, 99–100, 129
Muḥammad
  birth, childhood and life-work of, 80, 111–17; unity as great aim of, 29; proof of prophethood of, 30; conflicts following death of, 32 ff.; as messenger of God, 96; as victim of opposition and persecution, 119, 121, 142, 143; and the Qur'ān, 121–2; as terminator of prophethood, 140–1; need for acceptance of message of, 155–6
Mu'tazilites and miracles, 157

non-violence, Islam's policy of, 143–4, 147

omnipotence of God, 50, 124; man's delusions about, 63 ff.
opinion, Islam and independence of, 127

paganism, Islam as the uprooter of, 124–5, 144
parables, 31
persecution and opposition, Islam and Muḥammad as victims of, 119, 121, 142, 143
Persia
  conflicts with Byzantium, 109; Muḥammad's message and, 33, 143
philosophy
  and Islam, 37–8; its failure to bring assurance, 56
Plato, 38, 105
pleasure, Islam's attitude to, 145
prayer, 145

Index

pre-determination, destructive notion of, 63
prophets, the, 30, 31, 53; as helpers of man, 76–80; man's need of guidance of, 81–93, 106; healing powers of, 97; as God's messengers, 97; lesser intellects as aids to, 97; special attributes of, 99–100; rôle of, as guides, 100–4; and reason, 106; Islam's teachings on limited powers of, 124; and miracles, 157: *see also* Abraham; Jesus Christ; Moses; Muḥammad
proselytism, Islam's rejection of, 143, 144

Qur'ān, the
question of creation or pre-existence of, 29; teachings and interpretations of, 30–40; and divine inspiration, 118–22; on the 'friends of truth', 126; rewards of reading, 140; as revealer of Islamic virtues, 154: *see also* Muḥammad

rationalism, 71
religion and, 107–8; Islam and impediments to, 128
reason
and Islamic theology, 30, 31, 33, 34, 37, 39, 92, 126, 127; as parallel of the prophets' rôle, 106; camparison with religion, 107–8; as pioneer of authentic belief, 145
Reformation (Christianity), Islam's likeness to elements of the, 149–50
religion
man's lack of knowledge as bar to conviction in, 95; true function of, 103–4, 106–7; as source of discord, 104; as powerful force in man, 105–7; and reason and rationalism, 107–8; God's mercy towards diversities in patterns of, 130; and human progress, 132–41

religious tolerance, as Islamic policy, 143
revelation, the possibility of, 94–8
rich and poor, need for mutual charity between, 140
ritual, Islamic, 74

sainthood, pretensions to, 97–8
salvation, the prophets' rôle in, 106
science, 35, 38; the Qur'ān and manifestations of the universe, 39; as evidence of God's omniscience, 48–9, 54; man's labours in pursuit of, 70; prophets' guidance on, 103; scientists and objections to Islam, 153
sectarian movements, Islam and, 33, 151
self-discipline, man's need of, 69, 105
self-preservation, man's instinct for, 86
sense perception, 67, 92, 95
shī'ahs (religions sect), 33
Shirk as the supreme wrong, 63–4
simplicity of the Islamic faith, 145, 147
soul
man's incomprehension and concepts of the, 54; and man's sense of beauty, 68; concepts of immortality of, 81–2: *see also* after-life
suffering as source of good, 69
Sunnah, the, 35; and *Shirk*, 64
Syrians as converts to Islam, 33

taqlīd: see traditionalism
Tauḥīd, definition, meaning and source of, 29
theology, Islamic
history of, 29–39; dogmatic *Kalām*, 30; science of, 35
thought, Islam and independence of, 127
traditionalism
theologians and, 29; the Qur'ān's condemnation of, 40; as man's affliction, 66; Islam's campaign against, 126, 127
transcendence, doctrine of, 156

truth
  man's search for, 70, 92, 140–1;
  no room for divergence of mind on, 131

Umayyads, 33, 35, 144
unity
  as Muḥammad's great aim, 29;
  Islam as a religion of, 39, 123;
  as attribute of God, 51–2, 123–5

usury, Islam's attitude to, 140

Wāṣil ibn 'Atā, 34–5
will
  as theme of contention, 34; meaning of, 49–50; Islam and the freeing of man's will, 125, 127
wine, Islam's view of evil of, 140
wisdom of deeds and of God, 58–61
work, Islam's attitude to, 126